POLICY PERSPECTIVES

BROWN UNIVERSITY BICENTENNIAL PUBLICATIONS
Studies in the Fields of General Scholarship

POLICY PERSPECTIVES

BY

HENRY M. WRISTON

BROWN UNIVERSITY PRESS
PROVIDENCE, RHODE ISLAND
1964

COPYRIGHT © 1964 BY BROWN UNIVERSITY

All rights reserved

Library of Congress Catalog Card Number: 64-17776

To

RUTH E. SANDBORN
Colleague and Friend

Preface

THIS volume is a response to suggestions by a number of friends that I should give some account of my thinking about public policies since retiring from Brown University in 1955. The idea was to gather into one volume the major speeches (several never published) and various articles.

It transpired that their number and their bulk were both far too great. Therefore, these nine were selected as representative of talks to students, to The American Assembly, and to businessmen. Also included are three articles published in *Foreign Affairs*.

There is a strong temptation to "update" the material and make all expressed viewpoints consistent. That temptation was resisted; the only changes were to make printing style uniform. Thus errors of judgment—or, conceivably, prescience—stand out. The value of such a collection as this arises, at least in part, from exposure of shifting interests, emphases, opinions. I recall my sense of shock upon discovering that in the collected speeches of a public figure his errors of judgment had been edited out, but his accurate observations sedulously preserved.

I wish to express special thanks to Hamilton Fish Armstrong, Editor of *Foreign Affairs,* for permission to reprint three articles from that distinguished journal. All had profited by his wide knowledge and his critical sense tempered by his great kindness.

For help—far too feeble a word—in the selection of items, as well as for invaluable counsel in their original preparation, I am profoundly indebted to my wife. Her wide reading in literature resulted in many suggestions.

All the books I have published during thirty-five years, as well as innumerable speeches and articles, have benefited from the skillful editing of Miss Ruth Sandborn, a most highly valued research assistant who continued to provide editorial and other help even after I retired from Brown. This volume, like earlier ones, would not have been completed without her aid. Mrs. Dorothea Borden prepared the manuscript, and gave many other kinds of assistance, for which I am deeply grateful. I wish to express my gratitude to my successor at Brown, President Barnaby Keeney, for making their services available.

These are comments of a private citizen with no access to secret or confidential material. They are, therefore, the views of an individual helped by many, none of whom, however, shares any responsibility.

October 1963   HENRY M. WRISTON

Contents

I. Labels for People 1
II. Rugged Individualism 13
III. Education and the National Interest 32
IV. The Role of Higher Education in Furthering the Security of the Nation 56
V. Cultural Affairs and Foreign Relations 73
VI. Dawn Will Break: A Point of View on International Affairs 91
VII. The Age of Revolution 116
VIII. Thoughts for Tomorrow 139
IX. The Primacy of Secondary Consequences .. 166

I ∽ Labels for People

I WOULD like to talk with you about a man whom you know not at all, but whom I know reasonably well, namely myself.

I have been called a conservative. Indeed, the most distinguished book on conservatism in the United States links my name with that of Herbert Hoover. It would be hard to find a more authentic credential as a conservative than that. There was a time, not so long ago, when it would have been an insult to be so designated. It would have been almost like an accusation of moral turpitude. But times have changed somewhat; in any event, I do not resent that designation, for it expresses a simple truth.

In one sense, I am an involuntary conservative. My conservatism is the result of my training, for I was a historian. Any man schooled in a professional discipline bears the stigmata of his fundamental training, no matter what his subsequent experience may be. One can never fully escape the mold of mind that the discipline inculcates. A historian is not only consciously, but even more importantly, he is subconsciously aware of the weight and influence of the past upon the present. The philosopher George Santayana summed up the matter concisely: "Those who forget the past are doomed to repeat it."

Student Convocation, Brown University, March 1, 1961.

Hans J. Morgenthau in his book *The Purpose of American Politics*[1] puts it well: "Conservatism holds that the world, imperfect as it is from the rational point of view, is the result of forces inherent in human nature. To improve the world, one must work with those forces, not against them." A conservative knows that there is no real discontinuity in history, even when appearances would indicate a break, as for example in revolutions. Such violent changes as occurred in Russia in 1917-1918, and in Cuba in 1959, had their roots deep in the past. The apparent discontinuity is striking, but essentially superficial.

I once started a doctoral dissertation upon "The English Monarchomachs." They were men who denounced monarchy in the days of the Tudors. They rejected the doctrine of the divine right of kings; they developed anti-royal political theories. In some degree they prepared the way for the overthrow of monarchy, and for Oliver Cromwell and his Commonwealth. However, the weight of history and tradition proved too strong, and when Cromwell's iron grip was loosened, the monarchy was restored.

There is a mass of experience, an even greater weight of tradition, and a dynamism of habit by which the past, to some extent, dominates the present and shapes the future. Such tremendous forces cannot be shucked off as a garment.

Thousands and thousands of people in the Southern states know that the current relationship between the whites and the Negroes is wrong. Deep in their hearts they realize that in the fullness of time the present imbalance must be redressed. But the customs of the com-

---
[1] New York, 1960.

munity and the uncontrollable habits of thought and action arising from the past make the transition to a new attitude and a new relationship vastly difficult, and painfully slow. The Supreme Court in all its majesty may proclaim a change. It is possible, with great courage and effort and sacrifice, to produce token manifestations of the change that must come. But beneath, around, above, and beyond those tokens, there are forces that will not yield rapidly or readily.

George Meany regarded me as "timid" because the Report of the Commission on National Goals did not call for the complete integration of all schools at all levels during the sixties. The reason I was not ready to make such a statement was not timidity, but recognition of the depth of the prejudice, the force of the habits that must be overcome. Mr. Meany cannot even promise the end of labor union discrimination against color during this decade. I have no doubt of his sincere opposition to current manifestations of prejudice within some of the unions under his jurisdiction. I recognize that many unions have made progress in eliminating overt and palpable discriminatory practices. But he must be realist enough to know that even in the union movement this decade will not see the elimination of the evil. So far as education is concerned, he would seem to have preferred a strong, though ineffective, declaration. If wishes were horses, and pigs had wings, I would have joined him.

I have laid emphasis upon ingrained habits which affect reform adversely. It is essential to put equal stress upon the fact that not all past experiences or traditions or habits are bad. If they were, the condition of the world would be hopeless. If this were the first generation to have achieved insight into ethics, if we of the mid-twentieth century were the earliest discoverers of virtue, if all the saints and heroes of history had been ineffably stupid and blind, there would be little hope that we could make up for all past deficiencies within the short span of our lives.

A true conservative does not insist upon the *status quo;* much less does he seek to reverse the historical process and turn the clock backward. This remains a fact despite the assertions of columnists, commentators, soothsayers, and other wise men, who ought to know better, that such is the desire, intention, and effort of conservatives.

The function of the true conservative is to assess the historical situation with acuity and penetration. He must avoid starry-eyed optimism that would expect to brush aside adverse historical forces. He will retain from the past whatsoever things are true, whatsoever things are just, and whatsoever things are of good report. At the same time, he must energetically exploit the positive opportunities for improvement that experience and the dynamic of history make available. There are tides in the affairs of men which have their flood stages when reform can be carried forward with relative ease.

Yet another attitude is inculcated by the discipline of history. The historian knows that while there are certain cyclical characteristics in human experience, history never repeats itself. The historical process is not only continuous, it is unique. What has happened before is never precisely repeated. Change is partly dominated by momentum or inertia, and is partly subject to direction. The conservative utilizes the momentum, and alters the direction only moderately, knowing that his power will be stretched to its utmost to achieve even that much progress. He knows that if he tries to alter the direction too radically, reaction may well destroy his effort.

I do not hesitate to admit, therefore, that I am a conservative.

I have been called a liberal, and cannot deny the impeachment, if you so regard it. This word is abused almost as badly as the word "conservative." Rightly interpreted, a man is a liberal who makes its effect upon freedom the touchstone of the wisdom or the folly of a public policy. This is not the test normally applied today.

I am ready to accept the definition of the great Spanish historian-philosopher, José Ortega y Gasset: "Liberalism is that principle of political rights, according to which the public authority, in spite of being all powerful, limits itself and attempts, even at its own expense, to leave room in the State . . . for those to live who neither think nor feel . . . as do the stronger, the majority. . . . It is the right which the majority concedes to minorities."[2]

There is a tendency just now to make economic policy the acid test of a liberal. The "free spenders" of public funds are called "liberal," and the thrifty, "conservative." Whoever adopts that criterion accepts as gospel the statement of Stalin that "the material life of society . . . is primary, and its spiritual life secondary, derivative"; "one must look for the source of social ideas, social theories, political views and political institutions . . . in the conditions of the material life of society."[3] That is as illiberal a concept as could possibly be crammed into so few words. Yet unthinking people gulp down that Communist pill while verbally denouncing Communism.

We are deluged with statistics with regard to the growth of the economy, as though that were the true

---
[2] *Revolt of the Masses,* New York, 1932.
[3] This statement seems to me both so lucid and so fundamental that it will appear elsewhere in this volume.

measure of the health of the democratic process. It is not. I do not underestimate economic growth, or prosperity; they have values. However, prosperity and liberty are by no means identical—or even identical twins. Neither are they antitheses, though in some circumstances there may be tension between them, as when prosperity is made the supreme goal, even at the expense of curtailed freedom.

We are not hearing enough about the growth of freedom, and the right and the opportunity for every man to be aware of himself, to bend his mind and heart to the formidable task of self-realization. Facilitating that is the major obligation of government.

Arthur H. Sulzberger, the president and publisher of *The New York Times*,[4] wrote a letter to his own paper. Possibly he could not persuade his editorial writers to accept his view. He deplored one aspect of the proposed Franklin D. Roosevelt Memorial. I hope you have seen pictures of the prize-winning design for the memorial. It represents the sort of throwback to the past which ultra modernism so often achieves. It is a kind of synthetic Stonehenge proposed to be erected in Washington beside the tidal basin between the Jefferson and Lincoln Memorials. It consists of vast vertical entablatures—one at least ten stories in height—in something like the irregular circle of Stonehenge.

However, it is to be modern. Because the architects shun the vast labors of those Druids who presumably constructed the original Stonehenge, it is proposed to achieve the effect the easy way; concrete will be poured into forms. The uprights will be bigger, and therefore better, than the stones selected by the original Druid who

---
[4] Now chairman.

conceived what is now an ancient monument. The cement will have inscriptions incised upon it, drawn from what a cynic described as the ghost-written utterances of Franklin Roosevelt. Recalling the Athenians' altar to "an unkown God," this cynic would call these a memorial to an unkown author. Mr. Sulzberger made no such sardonic comment; he was protesting against the use of a famous passage embodying "the four freedoms." Let me quote him.

"What bothers me are some of the words that will undoubtedly be inscribed on these monstrous slates. Up to the time of Mr. Roosevelt, the First Amendment to our Constitution had provided four fundamental freedoms for all of us: Freedom of religion, freedom of speech, freedom of the press, and freedom of assembly. But at the apex of the dictators' power abroad, Mr. Roosevelt saw fit to drop two—freedom of the press and of assembly—and substitute instead freedom from fear and freedom from want.

"These are noble ideals, but why substitute? Why not add, why not have said that to our four fundamental freedoms we must now add these two new guarantees?"

I suspect that Mr. Sulzberger protested because he is a liberal according to my definition. The test—the ultimate test—of every political action is: Does it contribute to the growth of freedom, to self-awareness, and to the development of the individual? We are hearing almost nothing of these tests today.

Of all our political values, freedom is most easily mocked. A good example of such mordant mockery is Anatole France's biting remark that citizens live under the majestic equality of laws which forbid "the rich as well as the poor to sleep under bridges, to beg in the streets, and to steal bread." Ultimately, despite all distortions and all epigrams, freedom is not mocked. The first ten amendments to the Constitution have a greater validity today than when they were adopted. Associate Justice William J. Brennan, Jr. of the Supreme Court recently emphasized the need for alert defense of those amendments, now so often breached by state and local action.[5]

Beyond all else, I value the right to be myself. "For liberalism . . . is a fundamental idea about life. It is believing that every human being ought to be free to fulfill his individual and non-transferable destiny."[6] If that is *the* primary right, as I believe it to be, I have perfect justification for admitting the charge that I am a liberal.[7]

I have also been accused of being a radical, and I cannot deny it. In order to be a radical one must possess a certain naïveté. To college men, naïveté probably seems the ultimate in degradation. Yet I will not apologize. Did not the Great Teacher himself say, "Suffer little children to come unto me, for of such is the kingdom of heaven"? Was it not said much earlier, in the Psalms, "Out of the mouth of babes and sucklings hast thou ordained strength"? Of all the winsome characteristics of the very young naïveté is perhaps dominant. Children see some things directly and often observe truths more sophisticated minds do not perceive.

A proper measure of naïveté saves one from semantic confusions. For example, the Declaration of Indepen-

---

[5] *The New York Times,* February 16, 1961.
[6] Ortega y Gasset, *Invertebrate Spain,* New York, 1937.
[7] My chapter in *Goals for Americans* (New York, 1960) expands this view of the individual.

dence asserts that all men are created equal, and are endowed by their Creator with certain unalienable rights, among which are life, liberty, and the pursuit of happiness. I cherish the innocent faith that Thomas Jefferson understood the English language. Within the limits of his own experience I believe he meant those words sincerely, and expected them to be interpreted in their ordinary sense. I think he wrote them as the Oath of Allegiance says, "freely, without any mental reservation or purpose of evasion."

I believe with all my heart that all men are created equal. If you look at Asia, Africa—and the United States—it is clear that the expression of that belief is the most radical political and social statement a man can make. In a world just emerging from colonialism, dominated by prejudice, cursed with castes ancient and modern, filled with all kinds of divisive distinctions, that belief is radical.

A good many people stand up in church and recite a creed, no single statement of which they sincerely and unreservedly believe. They are paying a kind of tribute to the past; they feel that no one is cheated by their mental reservations. An enormous number of people read the Declaration of Independence in the same way. They mumble the phrases, paying not the slightest attention to the plain meaning of the words. Indeed, many regard anyone who does believe those words as subversive.

Recently former Dean Clarence E. Manion called me a socialist. I do not resent it, because among the other freedoms which I treasure is the freedom to be wrong. It is a freedom, I am bound to say, that I think he sometimes overdoes. He is not alone. Some years ago—while I was still at Brown—I was asked to lecture in Dallas.

The text[8] was read for me since I was in the hospital. Afterward, a prominent women's organization voted that I should never again be invited to their fair city because of the heretical views of a "leftist" speech I was supposed to have delivered there. Not to put too fine a point upon the matter, they did not like what I said—or rather what they thought I said, since apparently none of them heard or read it.

To return to my naïve approach, I can remember, as though it were yesterday, my first contact with a Negro. It is, indeed, one of my earliest recollections. My father and mother were entertaining the members of the Tuskegee Quartet in our home—certainly over sixty-five years ago. Up to that moment I had never seen a black man. When I was introduced and shook hands, I looked at my hand to see if any of the black had come off. It was a moment of chagrin for my parents; the situation was saved by the sense of humor of the singer, who smiled broadly and said, "Look again; it won't come off." That was my first experience with the social mixing of the races. As you see, it made an indelible impression on me. So when any person—white, or black, or brown, or red, or yellow, or any shade in between—is denied the equality with which he was born, I am outraged.

Can you find a better definition of a radical? It has nothing to do with communism, socialism, or any other ism. It does not even imply extremism. "Radical" etymologically has to do with roots; the root of the matter is a direct faith in the fundamental equality of men. It has somewhat the naïve quality that St. Paul exhibited when he wrote in his Epistle to the Romans: "The Spirit itself beareth witness with our spirit, that we are the children

---

[8] In *The Present Danger,* Dallas, 1953.

of God: and if children, then heirs; heirs of God, and joint-heirs with Christ."

Why have I engaged in this extended autobiographical analysis? It is not to defend myself, for none of you has attacked me. Moreover, I recall that a great president of Brown said, "Never defend yourself; your friends do not need it, and your enemies will not believe you."

My purpose has been to suggest that when you read in the paper about some person to whom, in his infinite wisdom, a journalist, probably a headline writer, has attached a label, you should not take it very seriously. Whether a man is called a conservative, or a liberal, or a radical, the label probably means nothing.

To begin with, it is not what the papers insist they give—an objective, unbiased account. Each of these adjectives is often used as a pejorative, and, in any event, each is so loose as to be dangerous for that reason alone. Their utilization is a failure of objectivity, for the adjectives are applied without study, analysis—or even more than passing thought. It subsumes a man under a label.

Even canned soup requires more than that. The Pure Food Laws demand the ingredients be shown. They are seldom simple. Let me read you the ingredients listed on a single can of Campbell's soup: beef stock, carrots, potatoes, tomatoes, onions, celery, peas, green beans, enriched spaghettini, vegetable oil, water (I was relieved to find that!), pea beans, salt, cheese, zucchini, sugar, bacon, cabbage, turnip greens, mustard greens, starch, monosodium glutamate, yeast extract, spice, garlic, hydrolyzed milk protein, and beef extract. Surely a human being is as complicated, and ought to have as much consideration given to his label as a can of soup.

You are, in fact, extraordinarily complex beings. If you do not know it, the faculty does. When anyone attempts to subsume any one of you under a single label, he is doing violence to truth, to justice, to wisdom, and, incidentally, to you. Every person, whatever his situation in life, is a vast mélange of ideas, notions, habits, energies, drives, inhibitions, impulses, controls, virtues, and vices. For though all men are created equal, each man is created differently, indeed uniquely.

The great human adventure is to "know thyself," and then to learn to be yourself. However fashionable, 99 44/100 per cent of the clack we hear about conformity is sheer nonsense. I was amused, just after preparing this talk, to read in a book review in *The New York Times*, "The denunciation of conformity has become a leading aspect of the new conformity everywhere." You could not really conform, no matter how hard you tried; I must admit some of you devote too much of your effort to that futile objective.

College is the place to abandon the effort to conform. Instead, make the effort to find out what within you responds to situations outside yourself. Cultivate those responses until they are characterized by skill, deftness, and above all else, by sincerity. Then you will be educated.

II ~ Rugged Individualism

There has been a whole spate of books, articles, and speeches bewailing America's lost leadership. Politician after politician cries out for "bold and imaginative" action—seldom defined at all and never with any precision. Religious leaders bewail moral decay, as preachers have since exhortation began; you can "read all about it" in the Old Testament. Publishers dominant in the field of mass media, who not so long ago called this "the American Century," now assert that we have lost our sense of mission and are lacking any faith in a national purpose. The wailing wall is crowded, and ululations fill the air. When one asks where new leadership is to come from, who is to define the national purpose, and who will summon us from moral lassitude, the answer is an embarrassed silence.

Recently there was a symposium on the national purpose. A number of people gave their view of what it had been, when it was lost, and what should be done to recover it. I found it intriguing that not one of the great minds even mentioned the individual and his responsibility. Every criticism was cast in collective terms, in terms of society.

This experience was a dramatic manifestation of the manner in which we have reacted away from the ideal

---
Bowdoin College, March 22, 1960.

of the individual living his life in an atmosphere of liberty and pursuing those inner satisfactions which Thomas Jefferson embodied under the word "happiness" in the Declaration of Independence. Happiness is a fascinating word; it was not a casual choice on the part of Jefferson. He did not say "pleasure" or "gaiety"; he did not say "diversion"; he did not say "leisure" or "recreation." He used a word deeper and more profound in meaning than any of those. Happiness is not the external pleasure that comes from wealth, diversion, distraction. It never comes to societies but only to individuals.

Moreover, we should note that Jefferson did not lump together the three values enumerated in the Declaration. Two of them, life and liberty, he spoke of as absolute. But with regard to happiness there was a vital qualification—the only right was the right of the individual to *pursue* it. The Declaration carried no guarantee of attainment of happiness. At the outset we might as well face the fact that many will pursue happiness with energy amounting to devotion and still not attain it. One may have life and liberty, yet still find only misery. There's the rub. Many have neither the will nor the courage to accept the challenge and pursue the good which life and liberty may make possible. They will ask a leader to take over the task and give them a free ride. But of that more in a moment.

There was a time when the individual was at the core of our political, religious, and economic thought. Indeed, the key to our history is the concept of freedom. One man may chase the dollar and consider it almighty. Thoreau could go to Walden Pond in search of his own goals; Emerson could exalt the thinker; Walt Whitman could extol the pioneers and assert that "the crowning growth of the United States is to be spiritual and heroic." Franklin, Jefferson, Edison, Theodore Roosevelt—and millions more—could follow their insatiable curiosity. Initiative is decentralized; responsibility is personalized; the individual is the ultimate value. His freedom is the key. Judge Learned Hand put the philosophy in a few words: "It is enough that we set out to mold the motley stuff of life into some form of our own choosing; when we do, *the performance is itself the wage*. 'The play's the thing.' "[1]

In far-off days we were not ashamed to speak even about rugged individualism. We respect men like Elijah Lovejoy, a Maine product, who lost his property and ultimately his life at the hands of a mob because he stood for principles. At the cost of life itself he would not surrender his opposition to slavery. We still pay him, and others like him, formal homage with ceremonies and tablets and prizes. But such heroes of the past do not seem very real to us. They are storybook men, or material for a television serial. Even in that medium it is the men of physical, rather than moral, courage who are depicted—or rather I should say romanticized. Some of you may have memories long enough to recall the Davy Crockett rage.

Somewhere in the 1930's, or thereabouts, rugged individualism became associated with industrial piracy, with defiance of moral checks, with exploitation of one's fellow men. If I may borrow an expression familiar in Britain, when we denounced rugged individualism we "threw the baby out with the bath water." We went too far, for nothing is more obvious than that leadership is a

---
[1] *The Spirit of Liberty, New York,* 1952. Italics supplied.

word which describes a quality of individuals, not of a society.

Surely the century which has known Woodrow Wilson, Lloyd George, Winston Churchill, Franklin Roosevelt, Charles de Gaulle, and Mahatma Gandhi should not find it difficult to realize that leadership requires not only individuals but rugged individuals. All those men were tried by fire; all came to power against striking odds. Indeed, if we look at the new nations of Asia and Africa, we shall find that a great majority of their leaders—like Nehru, for example—spent a good many years in prison. It was their courage and faith that inspired their nations.

There were other rugged individuals in this century, also, such as Mussolini, Hitler, Stalin, and, closer to home, Trujillo, Perez Jimenez, and more. Many of those rugged individuals were not, to put it mildly, on the side of the angels. Several were enemies of truth, peace, justice, and democracy. They attained power because they were more rugged than the defenders of those virtues. This was symbolized in history by the meeting of Chamberlain with Hitler at Munich; it was the rugged individual who dominated. One man was ready to take risks; the other sought to avoid them, and at too great a cost. He thought he had bought "peace in our time," but the gaily wrapped package contained war, not peace.

We have observed this same phenomenon in the United States. Senator Joseph R. McCarthy was a rugged individual. For a time it seemed that there were not enough individuals rugged enough to stand up to him. His power seemed too great to challenge. It was said so often as to put calluses on our ears that people dared not speak their minds in the face of danger to job, to reputation, and to family. That was doubtless true of those to whom security was the central goal of life, and, of course, some weak men responded with silence.

Amid the craven outcry of men who dared not face the "terror," recruitment for government service continued. Many public officials performed their reasonable service, ready to take the consequences. The best of them went on—if not serenely, at least with fortitude. Some who did suffered for it. That was tragic, but it established no precedent, for it had happened again and again in history. Many more went through the period of stress and strain unscathed, even as some do in battle. I find it extraordinary that we take battle heroes and heroes in public service in our stride, but we save our pity and our tears for civilian cowards.

If *Dr. Zhivago* could be written in the midst of Stalinism, it should give us some hint of the reservoirs of courage and integrity that can exist under circumstances that make McCarthyism pale by comparison. For every coward in the world, there is not only a hero, but a host of heroes. Recall what Boris Pasternak said when he was offered the Nobel Prize: the award "will never occur, since my government will never permit such an award to be given to me. This and much else is hard and sad, but it is these fatalities that give life weight and depth and gravity and make it extraordinary—rapturous, magical, and *real*."

Yet we were told that certain people would have said great and significant things if they had not been silenced by the terror of McCarthyism. My observation is that when he died and the terror was allayed, they still said nothing because they had nothing to say. I believe that for many he was a shield instead of a spear. He alibied the lazy and the timid from being exposed for what they were. I never knew anyone who had something significant to say who failed to say it because of McCarthy.

Once he was confronted by a Yankee individualist like Joseph N. Welch, McCarthy had met his match. Welch was not terrified. It took only one fearless, rugged individual, strategically placed at the right time, to show the hollowness of the McCarthy bluster.

The McCarthy episode was by no means the only instance where some quailed before an assault upon their security. It was merely a dramatic recent manifestation of a common phenomenon. Let us glance at some of the books which are supposed to reflect the current state of the public mind. One is about the "organization man," the man who suppresses his individuality or is so weak that others dominate it; he conforms to a pattern, as though he were made with a cookie cutter instead of being endowed with Godlike attributes. Another book talks of "status seekers," people who have no individual standards of value or the courage to assert them. They seek to promote their interests by identifying themselves with a "superior" social level. They want the sense of security which comes from standing in a mass of people where one is not conspicuous or cannot be identified except in relation to a chosen group.

This temptation to shed responsibility is not unique to our day or to this generation. Well over a century ago Alexis de Tocqueville, in his great work on democracy in America, discussed the nature of tyranny: "The will of man is not shattered, but softened, bent, and guided." The guiding will "enervates, extinguishes, and stupefies a people" who are "reduced to nothing better than a flock of timid and industrious animals, of which the government is the shepherd." In our own day the impulse to escape the harsh task of thought, to avoid responsibility, made "He will decide" one of the great slogans of the Mussolini era in Italy.

This passion for security and anonymity has not passed America by; as a great jurist said: "They are the defenses against the intolerable agony of facing ourselves. . . . We are in deadly fear of life, as much of our own American scene betrays."[2] To some extent because of eagerness to have others make the hard choices of life, there is loud complaint that "Washington does not give us leadership." But Washington in inhabited by individuals like the rest of the nation. If the goal of living is to hide in a social group, if we do not want to be rugged individuals, if we consistently decry individualism, why should we expect leadership? Whenever you sell individualism short, you lay the axe at the roots of democratic leadership, though you open the way for demagogues.

This recent denigration of the individual runs very deep and appears in unexpected and seemingly innocuous ways. For example, we demand guidance counselors in schools. There is nothing wrong with seeking advice or in having it available. Most of us can profit by good counsel from wise and disinterested persons. But what kind of guidance have they been giving? All kinds, of course; but it is writ large upon the record that counseling since the great depression has been predominantly defensive. This defensive character of counsel is one more evidence, among many, that though we have recovered

---

[2] Hand, *op. cit.*

from the economic and financial disasters of the thirties, the psychological damage has not yet been fully repaired.

For this reason, counseling has not been a summons to students to be themselves or to take the risks that go with rugged individualism. The slogan implicit in too much advice has been "safety first"; security is put before all else. Students are told to aim for certain jobs because there are plenty of vacancies and therefore not much danger of unemployment. They are advised to train for certain vocations because the pay is good, rather than because such employment of one's talents and energies brings intellectual, spiritual, and emotional satisfactions. This kind of defensive counsel will never help to produce leadership.

The Soviets are candid about their central doctrine. Whatever else they keep secret, this is no secret at all. Economic determinism is the professed key to their philosophy and to their policy. They say explicitly that "the source of social ideas, social theories, political views and political institutions" lies in "the material life of society." Communists are relentless in their logical defense of that concept, unswerving in their devotion to that idea. Such a doctrine is the complete denial of the historic American dream. It is the precise opposite of the great ideals which shaped American history, proclaimed with such eloquence by Thomas Jefferson in the Declaration of Independence.

Few Americans, therefore, would explicitly avow such a philosophical foundation for their way of life. Yet many, implicitly and in action, exemplify this grossly materialistic premise. Much of the recent advice to young men and women has been cast in the tone, the mood, and the framework of economic determinism. Amidst all the noisy chatter about resistance to Communism, there has been a silent surrender to one of its central ideas, namely the assumption that economic interest is primary, while other phases of life are secondary, derivative. Ironically, some of those who have shouted loudest about un-Americanism and Communist infiltration have swallowed this doctrine—and never felt it in the gullet as they gulped down this most un-American of all political and economic dogmas. They clasp Stalin's doctrine to their bosoms while with their voices they denounce him and all his works. If we have been blind to this fact, others have not. It accounts for the feeling often expressed in the new nations of Asia and Africa that there is little to choose between the avowed materialism of the Soviets and the unconscious materialism that they observe in the United States.

It is still true that life is more than meat and the body more than raiment. We can gain some insight into the proper choice of a life work by considering the word "vocation." Catholics use it in a particular sense, as a "call" or "summons," usually to the religious life. That is its root meaning and Catholics have no monopoly on it, nor do they claim to have. In customary use, however, the word has been emasculated; it means merely a regular job that will draw steady pay. It carries no sense of mission, no overtone of dedication; it is only a manner of making a living. As long as vocations are selected defensively, or because they are safe, or just because they carry material rewards, as long as their deeper nonmaterial satisfactions are sold short, the whole concept of leadership will continue to be sacrificed.

Ortega y Gasset said: "You are able to be whatever you want. . . . That is to say, among his various possible beings each man always finds one which is his genuine and authentic being. The voice which calls him to that authentic being is what we call 'vocation.' But the majority of men devote themselves to silencing that voice of the vocation and refusing to hear it. They manage to make a noise within themselves, to deafen themselves, to distract their own attention in order not to hear it; and they defraud themselves by substituting for their genuine selves a false course of life. On the other hand, the only man who lives his own self, who truly lives, is the man who lives his vocation, whose life is in agreement with his own true self."[3]

A guidance counselor who has made a fetish of security, or who has unwittingly surrendered his thinking to economic determinism, may steer a youth away from his dream of becoming a poet, an artist, a musician, or entering upon any other of thousands of careers, because it offers no security, it does not pay well, there are no vacancies, it has no "future." If we are to have guidance, it must not be the blind leading the blindfolded, but people with vision respecting not only the stars in the heavens but also the stars in the eyes of the young.

Among all the tragic consequences of depression and war, this suppression of personal self-expression through one's life work is among the most poignant. If you wish to speak in social terms, rather than in terms of individual self-expression, that suppression, when effective, is fatal to the concept of leadership. For leadership requires courage, boldness, and the willingness to accept risks. To use the most dreadful word permitted to be uttered in public, leadership inevitably, inescapably, involves in-

---

[3] *Man and Crisis,* New York, 1958.

security. Men who have no fear of damnation still tremble at that word—"insecurity." I suppose we should call it the modern substitute for the classic concept of Hell.

The retreat from the effort to stimulate leadership arises in part, also, from a profound misinterpretation of democracy. No political thinker of any stature in all history ever interpreted democracy as equality in all things. If you read the Scriptures, you will discover the parable of the talents—one had ten, one had five, a third had but a single talent. Read Plato and Aristotle and their successors; you can follow the idea down through the ages to Alfred North Whitehead. For example, Thomas Jefferson wrote: "There is a natural aristocracy among men. The grounds of this are virtue and talents." Nowhere among the great thinkers will you find anywhere an assumption that people are equal physically, mentally, or in terms of character. What you will find set forth as an ideal is that every individual, however broken his body or limited his mind, shall have equality before the law and equality of opportunity to fulfill his own highest potential. That is the American ideal.

In the reaction against rugged individualism, however, this historical and rational concept of democracy gave way to a sentimental and superficial idea that people should somehow be made equal in every respect. We can observe this effort all too clearly in education. During the last generation there has been a strong tendency to level requirements down, in order that the slowest, in the words of the sentimentalists, should not have their tender personalities "damaged by failure"—as though failure were not a normal experience of every human being.

The worst error which has bedeviled education during

this generation has been a tragic underestimation of the educability of individuals. Because of that error emphasis was too often transferred from learning to "adjustment" —a term more appropriate to a nut than to a person. In his book *Charley Is My Darling,* Joyce Cary made this profound statement: "Knowledge, in short the experience of the mind, is just as important to a child's happiness and 'goodness' as affection, adventure; above all, knowledge of his own moral position. And the last is often most difficult to come by, *not because he could not grasp a complex situation* ('this is a grand deed but a bad one') *but because grown-ups do not trust the power of his imagination to form a picture in more than one dimension.*"[4]

This doubt, this lack of trust in the individual, applies to all, but it is revealed most tragically in the treatment of the gifted. For, combined with the levelling process and interpreting egalitarianism as allowing no one an advantage, it tended strongly to suppress talents. Again, as in so many other ways, the whole concept of leadership was assaulted.

Realization that this was a cardinal error has, of late, been dawning upon many people. Now they seek hurriedly for some sovereign remedy for its dire consequences. Strangely enough, the beginning of wisdom in this respect is very simple. What the American student in secondary school and college needs more than any other single thing is, as I have already hinted, stars in his eyes. We have encouraged him not only to keep his feet on the ground, but also to fix his eyes on the ground. "Realities," so-called, rather than aspirations, have been offered him. But hopes, dreams, ideals—call them what you will—are prime essentials.

---

[4] New York, 1960. Italics supplied.

The second step in freeing talent for leadership is easy to state but will require heroic effort to bring to pass. It is to stimulate the student to summon the courage to follow his star and accept the consequences, joyous or otherwise, as events and his own will, energy, and skill may determine. Some will fail; some do even now amid this false concept of egalitarian adjustment. All will get hurt. That price—that price precisely—is paid by everyone who plays football. Is the realization of one's own being, or the fate of the nation, less worth the risk? In any event, no available cushion will avoid pain or death, for both are implicit in the human tragedy. On the other hand, many will find the happiness the Declaration of Independence said it was their right to pursue, and some will become leaders.

It was for such courage that William Faulkner made his eloquent appeal when he accepted the Nobel Prize. In a recent book Leon Howard[5] spoke of that speech as a "declaration of independence from the fears of the atomic age, designed to encourage young writers to cast off the bondage of fear." In the course of his response to the award Faulkner said: "I believe that man will not merely endure, he will prevail. He is immortal . . . because he has a soul, a spirit capable of compassion and sacrifice and endurance. The poet's and writer's duty is to write about these things. It is his privilege to help man endure by lifting his heart, by reminding him of the courage and honor and hope and pride and pity and sacrifice which have been the glory of his past. The poet's voice need not merely be the record of man, it can be one of the props, the pillars to help him endure and prevail." That is sound gospel, not only for poets and writers but also for men of every vocation.

---

[5] *Literature and the American Tradition,* Garden City, N.Y., 1960.

For a long time the Communists used a slogan: "Religion is the opiate of the people." Like most slogans it would never have gained currency, nor could it have been effective as propaganda, if there had been no shred of truth in it. But there was *some* truth. The Russian Orthodox Church had been corrupt; it had served the czar, often slavishly. It had tended to make people accept, rather than resist, a tyrannous regime. In that important sense it had indeed become an opiate.

With somewhat the same degree of validity it could be said that security has become the opiate of the people in America. This is not an assault upon all aspects of social insurance any more than the comment about one phase of the activity of the Russian Church is an attack on religion. No one in his right mind would wish to restore the ruthlessness of many phases of the Industrial Revolution. No one sensitive to humanity would yearn for some of the forms of capitalism which were common as late as the turn of the century. No one with any feelings would want the burden of unemployment to be borne by a man who found himself without a job through no lack of industry, character, or skill—that is, through no fault of his own. The system which laid responsibilities upon individuals without adequate resources to discharge them was wrong and had to be corrected.

It became essential for industry to recognize certain social obligations such as provision for retirement, sick leave, vacations, lay-offs, and severance pay. It became essential also for the state—society in its political form—to accept many responsibilities for social insurance, to participate in discharging obligations which could not properly be assigned to either the individual worker or his employer. The changes by which this alteration of emphasis was wrought proved to be a vast, though silent, revolution. It transformed the capitalism which Karl Marx observed; not only did it make many of his conclusions wrong; even more, it made them irrelevant. Failure to take this great revolution into account is what makes the Soviet view of American enterprise and American society so severely distorted.

Like so many essential reforms, the reaction against old evils sent the pendulum toward the opposite extreme. Reform went too far. "Security" became more than a proper and necessary buffer against misfortune. It was made an end in itself. There was a strong tendency to substitute too much public responsibility and promote too little private responsibility. When thus overdone, security became an opiate. Like other opiates, it tends to become an addiction.

Down on Cape Cod, where I live part of the year, we have people who work in the summer just long enough to make themselves eligible for unemployment payments. Then in the winter season they go on relief. Thus they avoid exposure to the elements and calm their consciences by saying that since they are paid X dollars for not working and since they would get only X plus Y dollars if they worked, their wages really amount only to Y dollars, an amount which is "obviously inadequate." That situation is not unique. In my own state of Rhode Island, it was discovered that public assistance checks were being sent to people who went to Florida for the winter season.

Some laws and some administrators have promoted this kind of abuse of sound protection. Let us pass over the needless cost to the taxpayer; let us not dwell upon the economic waste when there is so insistent a demand for more rapid growth of the economy. Instead let us concentrate upon one question: What is the effect of such habits upon the development of leadership? It can be summed up in one word: disastrous. You do not get boldness, or dedication to public service, or even responsible citizenship from those who choose as much idleness as possible as a way of life. They cease to be masters of the state, as the democratic thesis demands; they become its wards. When the citizen accepts the government as his guardian, democracy is in decay. A great Russian social philosopher pointed out that as "the state grew strong, the people grew weak." It will always be so.

In the American tradition poverty is regarded as an unmitigated evil. It is partly because this concept is so deeply embedded in our thought that we have made a fetish of security. Thus it has been said times without number that the poor cannot be interested in freedom, that democracy can flourish only among the relatively well-to-do.

All the evidence, when fairly examined, is against that shallow view. Our forefathers, who set our democratic pattern, were not leaders of a wealthy nation; far from it. And if wealth meant happiness, we, incomparably the wealthiest people in the world, should be correspondingly the happiest. But the weight of the evidence is to the contrary; if we are to believe our thought leaders—the columnists—we are not happy.

Denmark, where the average income is a fraction of that of the United States, is sturdily democratic. There the pursuit of happiness is almost palpable; one is struck not only at Tivoli but everywhere by the gift of laughter possessed by that people. Even in the midst of the German occupation they reacted more with mockery than with terror.

Ireland is almost a synonym of poverty; yet its dances and songs have a rhythm and a lilt that reflect innate gaiety. Their history is one of patriotism, of political passions that blaze into intensity. Nevertheless, their daily life, hard and often drab, is enlightened with a merry spirit. There, as elsewhere, democracy has flourished amid poverty.

If wealth and comfort and security are really the preconditions of the democratic process, we might as well write off Latin America, Asia, and Africa as ineligible to participate in democracy, and we shall soon be an island in the midst of a hostile sea of antidemocratic ideologies.

Even those who insist that the wealth and security we possess are the preconditions of democracy complain that the public is inert to its responsibilities. We are deluged with figures showing that a smaller proportion of the public vote in elections here than in countries where poverty is rife and security has not been made a fetish. We are told that Americans do not want to take the risk of running for office. More particularly, business leaders shy away from expressing opinions on public issues. Yet the same people who pronounce these strictures upon our citizenship, energy, and purpose still talk as though our major political objective should be more and more security. They do not see that the opiate has taken hold. Their only proposed cure for the addiction is larger doses.

Again and again you can hear news analysts on radio and television and often can read the commentators and columnists in newspapers discussing some topic. Then, in a rather awe-struck voice, they say that this policy or that action "involves risks." They speak of some statement or some person as "controversial." These comments are made in a tone that implies that risk is folly and that being controversial is equivalent to being wrong. Every time such a comment is uttered it is manifest evidence that security has indeed become an opiate. The democratic process requires controversy; and without risk there is no progress. The idle, the contented, the slothful do not crusade for advance.

Nothing in the Bill of Rights promises that the freedom there guaranteed can be enjoyed in comfort or in a serene atmosphere. In the long history of freedom, discomfort has always accompanied speaking on controversial matters. There never has been a time when there were not social sanctions against candor. But if freedom is to amount to anything, one must be ready to pay the price. When a man speaks out, he must be ready to receive, if not to absorb, criticism. Dostoievski lived in a land of tyranny; he knew its corrosive effect. With the wisdom that comes from lack of liberty, he asserted that "tragic freedom" is better than "compulsory happiness." It is a lesson we need to ponder.

Every aspect of life is touched with hazard; nor will all the political nostrums ever offered alter that fact. There is a deep insincerity in pretending otherwise. "Man always travels along precipices, and . . . his truest obligation is to keep his balance." "Life is our reaction to the basic insecurity which constitutes its substance."[6] Never was a profound observation stated with more simplicity and clarity. Even as we endlessly mouth "safety first" as our verbal motto, we build cars that go faster and faster. We undertake engineering feats that inevitably involve danger. If no risks are involved, the profits

---
[6] Ortega y Gasset, *The Dehumanization of Art,* New York, 1948.

of capitalism are vicious; they are nothing but usury or exploitation.

I am asserting that those who misrepresent the normal experiences of life, who decry being controversial, who shun risk, are enemies of the American way of life, whatever the piety of their vocal professions and the patriotic flavor of their platitudes.

All I have said can be summarized in a sentence. Life is an individual, as well as a social, experience; in the modern age there is no danger that you will escape social contacts and social pressure, but there is grave danger that you will lose the flavor and the joys which are inherent in the pursuit of happiness, one of your fundamental rights. The wisdom of the ancients was inscribed above the door of the temple of the Delphic oracle: "Know Thyself." Any wisdom that I have can be summed up with equal brevity: "Be Yourself."

III ∼ Education and the National Interest

THE profound involvement of the United States in world affairs raises many domestic questions, some at levels of deep significance. One, anxiously propounded, inquires regarding the adequacy of our education, both quantitative and qualitative, for our international responsibilities.

Though not generally differentiated, a number of quite separate issues are comprised in the question. One such is the cold war, now a decade old; many feel that education should take its direction from this central international reality in which the national interest is so deeply enmeshed that it should be the dominant factor in determining the content and emphasis of our educational system. On this assumption, there is an eager demand to know whether we are turning out enough, and adequately trained, experts in a wide range of skills essential to "success" in the cold war. The varieties of expertness required for international effectiveness are many; legal, economic, political, linguistic, scientific, engineering, cultural, and communication skills are all in demand.

FOREIGN AFFAIRS, July 1957. (Copyright 1957 by the Council on Foreign Relations, Inc., New York. Reprinted by permission.)

From the point of view of the national interest, all these seem to critics to be in very short supply. There are equal, and sometimes greater, doubts about another fundamental: the adequacy and quality of general education for international affairs. Are bachelors of arts and sciences ready to meet the citizen's obligation and participate effectively in shaping public opinion on world questions?

The most common measure of adequacy currently employed is the relationship between our educational product and that of the Soviets. Recently there has been an obsession with what the Russians are doing. In a report to the President, members of a special interdepartmental committee expressed their concern in these words: "Science and engineering have made such remarkable progress in recent decades that *the nation which holds the lead in those fields holds the initiative in world affairs*. Only at our great peril could we risk having leadership in basic and applied technology pass into the hands of our potential enemies."[1] This tone reflects a sharp reaction from earlier scorn of qualitative progress by the Soviets. For example, we badly underestimated their "mechanical ability"; it was said *ad nauseam* that Russian boys were not accustomed to strip and reassemble a jalopy, and that, as a consequence, Russia could not build and maintain an industrial society.

The superficiality, indeed the folly, of that misestimate of thirty years ago is now clear. Reacting from such extremes, we now tend to overestimate the Soviet Union just as badly, and feverishly seek to recruit scientists and engineers, not on the valid basis of fundamental interests and tastes, but to "keep abreast of the Russians."

---

[1] Italics supplied.

The educational program is judged in terms of a contemporary estimate of national security instead of the proper central objective in a free society—individual development. Again and again we are reminded that the Russian educational system is specifically designed, organized, and operated for the purpose of serving the national interest. This, we are repeatedly told, is one of the "advantages" of the totalitarians.

In these circumstances, the questions commonly posed are whether or not we are doing as much as the Russians, or doing what we do as well as they. As is usual, the mood of the moment can be "validated"; a flood of statistics is produced to convince us that we are doing neither so much nor so well. It is pointed out that Russian children go to school six days a week, ten months in the year. They are pressed harder to learn; they study under rigid discipline; more achievement is expected of them. Competition to gain the benefits of higher education—all at public expense—is exceedingly keen. Sardonic stress is put on a contrast in emphasis in matters of education. We live in a free, competitive society; yet competition, so conspicuous in many aspects of our lives, has been virtually abolished in education. That is why, we are told, the competitive spirit, banned from the classroom, has become so keen in athletics. In the Soviet Union, on the other hand, the economy is not founded on competition, but on central planning and direction. Education, however, is fiercely competitive; students know that progress upward is dependent on superior attainment and they exert themselves accordingly.

Russian students are accustomed to far more rigorous examination procedures than are common in the American educational system. In the United States, many enter college without ever having faced a long, searching examination. Soviet university students, therefore, are said to know more when they enroll, to study more intensively during their undergraduate years, and to be better equipped when they have completed their formal education.

So far as quantity is concerned, the Soviets are turning out more "engineers" than we are; often it is asserted that they are graduating at least twice as many. They are also training more "scientists." It is constantly brought home to us, also, that when Soviet citizens are sent abroad on diplomatic or technical missions they have had longer and better training in languages, in cultural appreciation, and in other aspects of education relevant to international service. No one who has the capacity and the will, and is ready to submit to the harsh political discipline of Communism, is denied the opportunity to fulfill his highest ambition for specialized training. If he succeeds in his university work, he can look forward to certain employment, distinctive social status, and unusually favorable financial recompense. If the process is not democratic in the sense that we understand the word, at least it is based on equal opportunity without prejudice of birth, parental occupation, or other irrelevance—save political conformity.

So runs the argument. The inference is that if the race is to the swift, the Soviets are surely winning it. If weight of numbers is to be decisive, the advantage lies increasingly with them. If thoroughness and expertness are the touchstones, it is agreed that Russia is producing first-class engineers, scientists, techicians of many kinds. That the best of them can do work of the highest caliber is made manifest in the scientific and technical publications which find their way to the West. It is even asserted that Soviet scientists are given more freedom to publish in some "sensitive" fields than many American research scholars, whose work is often blanketed under unnecessarily tight "security" arrangements. Soviet diplomatic skills are evidenced in the United Nations; American officials from several departments and agencies serving abroad are struck with the adaptability of Soviet representatives in many parts of the world.

In current comment the debit side of the Russian educational ledger is not heavily stressed. Yet it needs to be kept in mind. That serious unhappiness and unrest exist among Russian students is indubitable. The assumption, long accepted here as well as there, that perpetual and consistent indoctrination will condition the responses of students and effectively eliminate doubts and questionings, has not been borne out in practice. The role of students in the uprisings in Hungary and elsewhere makes the point explicit. Stubborn faith that the educative process will ultimately defeat efforts to confine it finds supporting evidence in the satellites, as well as in Russia itself.

When scholarly pursuits are carried to the higher levels, when the mind is challenged to new insights in science, to fresh boldness in technology, to appreciation of other languages and cultures, the inescapable result is to stimulate men and women to think for themselves. When Soviet-trained experts are sent abroad they see for themselves how false have been many of the stereotypes of the West which have been stressed in their school years.

Originality cannot be trammeled into offical channels; this basic truth should be enough, by itself alone, to suggest the folly of shaping the content and emphasis of education to conform with an officially defined "national interest." Opening higher education to more and more youth is like opening Pandora's box; while some wills can be curbed and many skills controlled, the human spirit is such that the more original and constructive individuals will seek freedom, not merely as one satisfaction among many, but as an absolute necessity. The very scope and sweep of the Russian educational effort may well hasten the kind of evolution in the Soviet system for which we all hope.

In any event, it does not make sense to count noses of graduates and treat the resulting figure as a reliable index of growing strength or increasing weakness in the specific field tested. Many who are called "engineers" in one country might be called "draughtsmen" in another; labels never accurately reflect the content of education; for comparative purposes as between two disparate societies they are totally unreliable. Far more important than crude numbers is the use to which experts are put. The United States uses a very large percentage of its trained personnel in the production of consumer goods; the Soviets virtually starve consumer industries of such personnel. If we are considering the "usefulness" of expert training for employment in international affairs, the distribution of trained talent is more significant than the raw numbers produced.

More important still is the degree to which experts persist in their occupational commitment. It is said that by the time they are fifteen or twenty years out of the universities perhaps two-thirds of the Americans classed as "scientists" or "engineers" have shifted their occupations to posts where their technical training is not of immediate use. That is one of the characteristics of a free society;

a man is free to choose his vocation not only at the beginning of his career, but at any stage thereafter. Continuance or change may be motivated by an almost infinite number of factors. As long as so large a proportion of specially trained men and women leave the area of their expertness, it is hard to make a convincing case that there is a serious "shortage." It indicates, at the very least, that the best attack on the problem does not lie in producing more people with a superficial or unstable vocational commitment.

High-pressure campaigns to recruit students for a scientific—or any other—career in order to serve the national interest may merely increase the number who later become dissatisfied with their impulsive choices and leave the fields in which they were trained in search of more congenial or more financially rewarding occupations. Any attempt to alter this situation by legislative and administrative action would constitute a revolution in American life. Even before the lapse of time which brings disillusionment to so many persons with specialized skills, large numbers of them are at work which does not fully—or even significantly—employ those skills. A great deal of specialized training is used inefficiently or wasted as a result of inadequate job analyses and poor personnel techniques.

We have no reliable information with regard to either of these two situations in Russia; we do not know how fully available skills are exploited or how large a percentage of trained people persist in their specialized lines of endeavor. The lack makes comparisons almost, if not quite, worthless. In most recent discussion it has been taken for granted that the Soviets do better in these respects than we do, but solid evidence to support the assumption has not been forthcoming.

Part of the American thesis is that, even tested by the national interest, the free and voluntary acts of individuals will, in the long run, lead to more productivity and better results than the directed activities of people, however well-trained, who must be politically obedient and do as they are told, accepting assignments which may be distasteful. It must be conceded that we do not have objective proof that this is true in the short run; the totalitarians, whatever the color of their shirts—black, brown, or red—have had striking successes in diplomacy, in finance, in manufacture, in technological and scientific progress.

It seems likely that where men have never known freedom, as in Russia, and where the state has always had a dominant place in education, the adverse results of directed activity are not nearly so serious as we who take freedom for granted would expect. Count Sforza, in exile from Fascist Italy, like others who fled Hitler's Germany, lamented the readiness of intellectuals of many sorts to knuckle under to dictators and serve totalitarian states with fidelity and skill.

The traditions of education in this country where official control has been almost unknown evoke a different reaction. This is why loyalty clearances, and the uproar over persons who have been denied such clearance, have produced an adverse effect upon the readiness of scholars, students of diplomacy, linguists, scientists, and technologists at the higher levels to turn their energies to government programs.

Freedom, voluntarism, and self-direction are settled habits with us. When customary modes of work and thought are disrupted by the injection of political questions, the results are adverse. When the availability of individuals for government service is obstructed by overelaborate loyalty and security procedures, many men, accustomed to the free atmosphere of universities, are repelled. The type of school required for specialists in cultural, linguistic, economic, political, and communications fields has long set its own patterns of work and standards of accomplishment without governmental monitoring; when that appears, it is found exceedingly irksome. So long as individuals have complete freedom of choice as to the direction of their energies, they will tend to seek posts where their employment will not be postponed for months waiting clearance, where they do not have to be concerned lest some word misunderstood, or some earlier association, can be exploited to their perpetual embarrassment.

On the other hand, Russians who have assented to political conformity as the price of specialized education, who go to universities in the expectation of being directed after graduation, do not have the same resistance to the management of their careers as do Americans. It is the more readily accepted inasmuch as other avenues of employment do not stand wide open to them as is the case with specialists in this country.

Even in this matter, however, we should be wary of confusing the short run with the long pull. Overextended as the tenure of the totalitarians seemed to us, the black-shirt and brown-shirt dictators did not last long enough to test the ultimate consequences. And the red totalitarians have only relatively recently been accelerating their educational programs and sending large numbers of experts abroad; we do not yet have conclusive evidence that Soviet faith in directed effort will succeed, just as we do not have definitive proof that our confidence in freedom will be fully vindicated in this particular area. However, there is much positive strength in our educational tradition. The base upon which higher education rests is broader in the United States than in any other nation in the world, including the Soviet Union. If, under our system, we do not subject the young student to such rigid discipline and urgent pressure to learn, much is done outside school to stir his imagination, to encourage self-reliance, to stimulate originality and individuality of approach.

Undisciplined election of subjects is predicated upon the assumption that the fruits of free minds are both more varied and more valuable than the products of like minds moving under rigid control. Again and again foreign visitors testify to the superior responsiveness of American students. Coming to the United States in a highly censorious frame of mind, they not infrequently comment upon the eagerness, the critical temper, and the self-reliance of American students. Educators have long held that these qualities constitute a vast natural resource.

This much more can be said: there is almost no special skill, of whatsoever kind, that cannot be developed in some institution within the United States. Where such training is given, the facilities of library and laboratory and the availability of competent instruction cannot be matched anywhere else in the world. This applies to linguistic, literary, and cultural subjects, to economics, politics, history, philosophy, as well as to science and technology. The range, the depth, and the quality of specialized training available at some institution, or in many, are no less than astounding.

The size of the United States, the enormous variety in the patterns of institutions of higher education—in how they are controlled and supported, in their equipment and standards—sometimes make it difficult to identify precisely the place where the individual can best fulfill his intellectual and vocational objectives. Nevertheless, so far as concerns the acquisition of expertness in almost any imaginable field which can be of national service, the graduate departments of our universities can meet the demands put upon them.

Limitation upon the numbers of highly trained individuals does not arise primarily from lack of facilities or space or equipment. Naturally every institution is ambitious—and rightly—to have larger quarters and better equipment and more books. In their clamor for these desirable things they often make it appear that what they now have is "totally inadequate." By utopian standards, to which every good institution aspires, it is. In comparison with the rest of the world, however, the standards of university living are as superior as other phases of our living standards. More important than any physical lacks, so far as producing specialists is concerned, are deficiencies arising from inadequate preparation of applicants for admission. That difficulty begins long before the universities have any direct responsibility.

This leads to the consideration of another basic question, namely, whether we are supplying our society with college graduates who possess the knowledge, the point of view, and the mental approach to international relations which will make them good citizens of the world as well as of the United States.

Basic to any useful thought about this matter is the remembrance that education is, in two senses, a long-term enterprise; programs to deal with fundamental national interests cannot be extemporized. In the first place, what the student can do in college depends, to a large extent, upon his earlier experience. Decisions taken inconspicuously and separately in a great many places affect that experience; in numerous instances they are not observable until years later. In the second place, the value for citizenship of what a student gets out of his undergraduate years does not become apparent in any decisive way for another ten to twenty years when his personal responsibilities have come to maturity. Taking these two factors into consideration, there may be a lag of twenty to thirty years before trends and their consequences are perfectly clear. This is why crisis psychology and crash programs, to which we are so prone, do not constitute a wise approach to cold war problems.

Current confusions and frustrations are the fruit of old misestimates as to what needed to be known. Decisions made long ago with almost no public notice have produced some seriously adverse consequences. The damage done cannot be repaired in an instant; "intensive" programs, so often suggested to "cure" some deficiency, are bound to fail. This point is so fundamental that some background is desirable.

In the year 1940 an impressive list of names associated with education was attached to a pamphlet published by the American Council on Education, the most widely recognized organization dealing with the total educational program. It was called *What the High Schools Ought to Teach*. Its substance was of great importance; its tone was even more significant. It regretted even the modest amount of mathematics taught, and even the teaching of precise English, on the extraordinary ground that these were "difficult" subjects. They were described as "stumbling blocks"; insistence upon meeting standards of lucid and effective English and upon reasonable mathematical literacy had the effect of driving students out of school and thus were undesirable. The study of foreign languages was seriously deprecated; a "course in general language" was suggested as a substitute. As for science, "only a few pupils need advanced mathematical physics." Every established study had to face a "pragmatic" test: "What's the good of it?" All too often the "good" had to be tangible and marketable.

The pamphlet was saturated with the dejected spirit engendered by the depression. At that time, it was held that Hitler's rise was aided by people educated beyond their opportunities; many saw a like situation coming to dominate American education. There were not only "too many" engineers and scientists; too many young people were going to college. High school had been raising too many "white-collar" hopes; fear was expressed lest in the backwash of unemployment youth become disillusioned with the American system and fall prey to Fascism. In "the statistification of a mood," figures were produced to "prove" that we faced a dangerous intellectual glut. This mood prevailed long after the depression which occasioned it was gone. As late as the spring of 1950, government statistics led to a prediction that only half the graduating engineers would find employment; thereupon applications for admission in that field fell off sharply. At the same time it was "proved" that there was a "surplus" of high school teachers. Transient situations were projected into the future.

The pamphlet on *What the High Schools Ought to Teach* did not raise a storm because it was not nearly so much a new program as a rationalization of what had already been spreading through the school systems during the depression. When the Second World War ensued, it was discovered, to the horror of the armed forces, that the level of mathematical literacy was far lower than it ought to be. The reason lay in the persuasiveness of the point of view expressed in a pamphlet of which the public had heard little or nothing. Mathematical requirements had been whittled down so far as to produce results adverse to the national interest, not to speak of the intellectual impoverishment of unnumbered individuals. The pamphlet which symbolized and stimulated this drift failed to lay emphasis upon the almost magical effect which better teaching could have produced both in the use of our mother tongue and in one of the most precise instruments of human thought. All its emphases were negative; small wonder the consequences were also negative.

Furthermore, a slogan was current a quarter of a century ago: "The failure of the student is the failure of the teacher." This crisp aphorism may have been intended to stimulate better teaching. If that was the purpose it backfired badly. In any event, it did nothing to stimulate better study; it was carried to such an absurd extreme that the grade of failure was actually abolished by official decree in a great many communities across the country. Frequently all grades were abolished lest they stimulate competition.

The effect was to relieve the individual student of basic responsibility for his own performance. Through a complete misinterpretation of democracy—a substitution of equal treatment for equal opportunity—the practice of speeding the bright student along at his best pace and letting the slow student take more time to master the fundamentals was virtually abandoned. Adapting the educational pace to the capacities of the individual was thought to develop a superiority complex in one group and an inferiority complex in the other.

These and many other decisions, no one of which was dramatic in itself, no one of which was imposed by federal or even state authority, infiltrated many school systems. Taken together, these separate decisions led to averaging down the quality and quantity of instruction until the bright were often bored and the zest for learning was sometimes impaired for those best equipped by mind, by motive, and by character.

Linguistic competency, so important for our current world responsibilities, deserves a special word. Paradoxically, when the United States had few contacts abroad, language studies flourished; as our world-wide contacts multiplied, linguistic competence waned. In an emotional binge during the First World War, German was dropped from many schools. There was a switch to Spanish, partly because it was thought to be "more valuable" in our dealings with Latin America, but also because it was "easier." The teaching of French never gained great momentum. The suggestion that Russian should be taught would have been greeted with horror. On the grounds that Latin and Greek were difficult and not "useful," they disappeared from nearly all curricula. Were they not dead languages of vanished civilizations? What was their relevance for the new world of today? The abandonment of the ancient languages, with their great emphasis upon grammar, upon vocabulary, upon exactness; prejudice against German; and the denigration of precision in the use of English produced conspicuous linguistic deficiences long before the time came for students to enroll in institutions of higher education.

To compound these deficiencies, the laws of many states required publicly-supported institutions of higher education to admit any graduate of a high school within the state. Since graduation became more and more a matter of spending a specific number of years and less and less learning a defined quantity of knowledge, and qualitative achievement was discounted, many institutions of higher education were almost swamped with poorly prepared undergraduates whose objectives were social rather than intellectual and whose habits were far from industrious. So serious did this situation become that in many institutions at least one year, and often a second, came to be devoted to repairing the deficiencies produced by the soft techniques of precollege education.

If one dwelt too long upon the various adverse factors in preparatory education, the result would be complete discouragement. Two reasons exist for reaching a more optimistic conclusion. The first has to do with the total environment of American youth. Their habits of mind and action are shaped by many experiences outside school; not all such factors are positive, but most have been predominantly so. This accounts for the independence of mind and freshness of approach which foreign visitors have so often noted.

The second favorable factor is that because of the almost complete decentralization of responsibility many school systems never followed the fads but kept a steady educational course. Moreover, in places which softened their programs scandalously some of the bad educational practices have been reformed. There is, for example, a renewed emphasis upon the gifted student. The long decline in mathematics has been reversed and the subject again is treated as important. Languages, likewise, are receiving more stress. The intellectual disciplines are regaining their lost position; some of the "design for living" emphases are giving way to more substantial study. The fashion for extremes in the absence of discipline has passed. The fruits of these reforms are showing in the improved quality of students applying for admission to strong institutions.

Furthermore, the tone of official utterance has changed. In the interdepartmental committee report to the President this is conspicuous. For the first time in many years an official document has laid great stress upon better teaching, upon mathematics and other basic disciplines, and upon early identification of and more attention to the students with outstanding talent. There is fresh and welcome recognition that the problems are complex and must be attacked "on many fronts" and with the realization that the long-range approach is vital.

By no means all the difficulties of higher education in the preparation for world affairs stem from shortcomings of the secondary schools. The colleges were swamped by the tremendous expansion of knowledge in the last half of the nineteenth and the first half of the twentieth centuries. The progress of science, the diversification of economic studies, the expansion of anthropology, social psychology, sociology, and other disciplines created problems novel in dimension. Many kinds of specialism invaded the liberal arts program; professional groups forced preprofessional preparation back into the college years.

So great was the glut of courses that many institutions all but abandoned the idea of organization within the curriculum. What had once been an "elective system" among very limited choices was now applied to a vast array. Each course was taught from its own point of view and without much relationship to the content or method of any other. Students often made their elections on whims—on the time of day the class met; whether it met on Saturdays; for vocational reasons, real or fancied; and upon every kind of irrelevant or trivial impulse—as well as upon sound and well-considered grounds.

It was during this time, and in these circumstances, that international relations began to be regarded as of great importance for the United States. Concern was expressed lest we produce "international illiterates." In the attempt to edge into an already overcrowded curriculum, international relations suffered because it was not a "discipline"; that is to say, it had no well-defined corpus of knowledge and no recognized mental mode of approach to its mastery. Outside academic circles that may seem a trivial barrier.

Nevertheless, in the college context it proved serious; an inchoate subject was brought into competition with well-defined, long-established disciplines. History, for example, has a characteristic content and an identifiable method of approach to its mastery. So also has science. So, at one time, had economics and political science. But international relations as a study is compounded of history, politics, economics, diplomacy, strategy, cultural appreciation, and a dozen other identifiable but complicated subjects. It did not fit neatly into any curricular position; it seemed to trespass upon established fields.

In consequence, the new subject worked its way into curricula like a wedge. Early courses tended to center upon international law, reflecting a hoped-for extension of the idea of a "government of laws, not of men" into international life. It accorded with the American enthusiasm for the Hague Conference and the establishment of a "world court." It overestimated the number and importance of the matters which opposing parties would agree to regard as justiciable.

The First World War brought disillusionment with international law. The Paris Peace Conference, the formation of the Council of Ambassadors, the League of Nations, and the new World Court centered emphasis upon structures for peace. Accordingly, there ensued a spate of courses on international organization. Ultimately the refusal of the United States to join the League of Nations, and then the failure of the League itself, temporarily lowered the level of the popularity of such courses. The establishment of the United Nations and the application of Madison Avenue techniques in "selling" it to the American people led to a renewed emphasis upon international organization.

Meanwhile, stress shifted to courses in diplomatic history. They often seemed to put the United States in the center of events in which its activity had, in reality, been peripheral; they were marked by the lack of objectivity and catholicity of outlook which so annoys Europeans. Moreover, instruction regarding large parts of the world, such as Asia and Russia, was, to put it mildly, meager. With the decline and often the virtual disappearance of language requirements, the range of materials available for reading purposes was narrowed to English. Because relatively little of vital importance was in English, reading was still further narrowed in many institutions to textbooks; they have been well described as "condensed summaries of oversimplified, predigested information without intellectual challenge." Many were more nearly purveyors of dogma of one brand or another than enlightening expositions.

The Second World War again called attention to the serious deficiency in the knowledge of language and the inadequacy of language by itself without understanding the culture it expressed. Area-language studies were undertaken under Army leadership, using intensive methods and new linguistic techniques. For the most part the vogue did not survive in undergraduate studies long after the war. So serious is the weakness in this field that of the many thousands who take the examinations for the Foreign Service only a very small percentage can pass a language test of moderate difficulty. In consequence, serious language training must be undertaken for the majority after their appointment.

The cold war led to a strong revulsion from interpretations of international events in terms of law and morals. Instruction tended to make geographical and power considerations paramount. As a result, there was a good deal of emphasis upon geopolitics; the dogmas of Sir Halford Mackinder and his followers were accepted rather uncritically. The "realists" who made power the touchstone of reality did almost as much damage to the understanding of international affairs as the sentimentalists had done at an earlier time.

Throughout the entire period there were some courses in current events, often carried under such pretentious titles as "World Politics." On the whole they were discursive and superficial. During the First World War, for example, Stoddard and Frank's *Stakes of the War* became virtually required reading for most college students. It was meager fare, indeed, and far from scholarly. It was part of a tendency towards teaching international relations "for a purpose," in short, indoctrination. It is a tendency which has never been completely rooted out.

This sketch of the way in which the subject edged into the course of study illustrates two things. First, different phases of an ill-defined "national interest" led to successive emphases in instruction. Second, the development of courses revealed the fact that international relations are exasperatingly complex. Nearly every scholastic discipline in the whole academic gamut makes an impact upon their understanding. There is a tendency, at the present moment, to think that, so far as international relations are concerned, the importance of science is new. This is not true. The coming of gunpowder was scarcely less revolutionary in its day than the atom in our time. It required a complete revaluation of strategy and tactics and altered the balance of power decisively. In international relations such considerations cannot be overlooked.

Clearly the teaching of international relations requires a vast range of mental processes and assessments of values. In order to "understand," the student must become a competent amateur in many disparate fields of knowledge. The effort to oversimplify, to choose a key subject, or to predigest everything into a ready-made synthesis requiring no urgent or painful effort on the part of the student will do more harm than good.

What conclusions can we draw? First, since it is a long-term enterprise, education that takes its cue from the current situation is obsolescent even before the student who has been exposed to it graduates.

Second, there are goals and values not only more significant but more valid than competition with Communism. There is something inherently absurd in the demand that we "recover the diplomatic initiative" while surrendering the educational initiative to the Soviets, making crude comparisons with them the test of educational success or failure.

Third, we must cease to think of education as stuffing the student, by the age of twenty-one, with enough knowledge to last him the rest of his life. This is an unreal but a persistent expectation. It accounts for the tendency to regard the number of courses offered as a test of an institution's effectiveness. This false faith in bulk also explains that hardy perennial in Congress—"A West Point for Diplomats"—as though the main reliance of the Army for general officers was upon what cadets learned there rather than their growth through experience and in the many post-graduate schools to which military officers are sent. There should be much less stress upon what the student is taught and what he knows at the age of twenty-one than upon his capacity to find out, to think about what he knows, to organize it usefully in his mind. Above all, we should cultivate the zest and zeal to continue to learn through independent study and reflection. Indoctrination achieves no useful purpose; it seeks to close the mind. What is needed in a world changing as fast as ours is flexibility in approach and power of thought.

Fourth, so far as the undergraduate course is concerned, the broader the acquaintance of the student with the fundamental disciplines in the humanities and the social studies, the better equipped he is likely to be for understanding international problems. In most colleges it is better not to have an undergraduate department of international relations, but to rely upon an interdepartmental field of concentration.

Fifth, for those who want careers abroad or wish to

be professional students or practitioners of international relations, graduate study is essential. No one in a world as wide as ours can be a specialist in everything, and the universities have done well to distribute among themselves, by a process not entirely rational but nevertheless practical, the many specialized studies. There are several distinguished centers for the study of Russia, its language, culture, tradition, economics, history, strategy, and diplomacy. There are four or five which deal with the Far East, more particularly with China. Still others are concerned with the Middle East or Southeastern Asia or Africa. The Indian subcontinent has itself become a field of specialization. There are good courses of study on Latin America and on Eastern Europe. There are almost innumerable graduate courses in law, diplomacy, and international economics. There is, in short, an extraordinary range of opportunities for a graduate student to acquire specialized knowledge.

Finally, it must be remembered that in the United States extracurricular interests are often a very potent educational force. For many years there have been international relations clubs, forums of various kinds, and a host of other voluntary activities which have stimulated interest and awakened the students' desire to know about international affairs. Not to be overlooked are the informal contacts of undergraduates with foreign students registered in our institutions. Many assign to such contacts a great influence in evoking interest in world problems. All these voluntary, noncurricular associations are particularly valuable because they lay the foundation for maintaining a concern for international relations after graduation. They lead to participation in the almost infinite number of voluntary activities which are so characteristic a feature of American life.

American education is the responsibility of communities, of states, of private organizations. As a consequence, there is a variety of approaches to every educational problem which is bewildering to all but long-time students of the American scene. To minds that overemphasize "order" and to those that admire foreign educational practices, the variety will be called "chaotic"; to others it seems full of opportunity. In so complex a situation no "direction" can be established save by public opinion operating in many ways and in many places. Also no generalization can be made to which exception cannot be taken. Nevertheless, considering the relative newness of the United States as a major World Power and considering the problems which institutions have faced in incorporating not only international relations but a host of other new subjects into their courses of instruction, the results have been good.

IV ~ The Role of Higher Education in Furthering the Security of the Nation

WHAT can higher education do to further the security of the nation? How does one set about designing a program to educate for the kind of world in which we must live out our lives? It must be admitted that there is confusion on this point. So much energy has been spent in perfecting specific techniques that inadequate attention has been paid to a coherent design for the whole.

A philosopher offers a key to the puzzle. In *The Aims of Education and Other Essays*,[1] Alfred North Whitehead gave a hint so basic that it is almost never mentioned; nevertheless it furnishes the text for all I have to say. He used four short words: "The students are alive."

Before impatience with so obvious a comment closes your minds to the full implication of the phrase, give it enough analysis to see why one of the intellectual geniuses

---

Sesquicentennial of the United States Military Academy, West Point, March 5, 1952. An excerpt.
[1] New York, 1929.

of our time thought it worth while to set down a patent truism in a book on education.

What is the meaning of "alive"? To begin with, I should not include the chicken heart that Alexis Carrel and his associates kept "alive" for a number of years after it had been removed from the chicken. Presumably that was an experiment of great scientific importance, but it involved a definition of the difference between "life" and "not life" far too tenuous to be applicable to a discussion of education. Life, surely, means growth, change, response to pressures—atmospheric and many others. Such a description, however, might apply to a tree; something more vital must be inherent in the assertion that students are alive.

Fundamental is the capacity not only to grow physically but to gain appreciation and understanding of one's environment. More important is a constantly enlarging ability to reshape the environment—imaginatively, purposefully, and skillfully. Man alone can do these things; that gift sets him apart from all other creatures; it clothes him with human dignity. In attaining these goals he reaches his highest potential, manifesting not alone power but wisdom. That word should not be slurred over: wisdom. No wonder it is exalted in the Book of Proverbs: "Wisdom is the principal thing; therefore get wisdom." Its possession is essential to the fulfillment of life's promise.

This quality of being alive varies greatly in intensity. For a newborn child the zone of awareness is extremely limited. He has no experience with hearing; therefore sounds give him only a minimum of information. His power of communication is severely limited. His eyes do not focus, his sight is dim; he sees little and what he sees does not signify much. As the area of awareness widens and deepens, life takes on new dimensions. During the first year or two the change is so swift and dramatic that it seems like a miracle. If education performs its mission, growth is continuous throughout life. Failure steadily to broaden and sensitize consciousness may fairly be described as an assault upon the life principle itself.

Of what does awareness consist? In one sense, we all see the same things, but some pay no more heed than as if they were blind; others give them full attention. If we break "attention" into two words, its meaning becomes clearer: "at tension" a person feels the pull of the object at which he is looking. "Feels the pull of the object" surely signifies something more than mere awareness of its presence; it means the object enters fully into the observer's knowledge and becomes an integral part of his life. If the object is not physical, but intangible—an idea—the sensitivity which feels its pull requires more rigorous discipline for its attainment than awareness of a pretty girl, let us say. The idea may be even more beautiful, if not so obvious in its power to attract.

Life's great adventure lies in steadily extending the range of observation, deepening the sense of awareness, filling in the pattern of meaning, not alone during the period of youth, but throughout the whole of life. That provides ever fresh experiences of mind and body; one becomes more and more alive—more alert to what occurs in the world, more responsive to beauty, more perceptive of significance, more sympathetic—more wise.

The first obligation of the educator, therefore, is so to teach, both through the choice of materials and by his method, that every student is stimulated to full aliveness and habituated to reflection, by which observation takes on meaning and enters into mature experience. Teaching has never been subjected to such scientific analysis as might make it possible to set a standard pattern for every teacher. Indeed, it is doubtful that such a goal is desirable, for teaching is in truth an art. It requires freshness of insight and individuality of approach. Standardization destroys both. Both can be improved by rigorous self-discipline. As in other arts, there are great practitioners; there should be many more.

As yet we have no idea how far, by the efficient management of time and energy, teachers could expand the quality of the student's life, as scientists and doctors have extended its length. That is not an indictment, for the secrets of the wonder drugs are relatively simple compared to solving the riddles of student motivation. Difficulty should spur us on, because anything less than great teaching impairs the life of a student. Stated in physical terms, it cripples him—an effect which would be considered barbarous, if we were not so accustomed to it. It disregards the faith and promise of the Declaration of Independence, in which life is put first, before liberty.

Every study of the adult learning habits of the alumni of American institutions of higher education offers clear evidence that after graduation many of them cease to widen their interests or intensify their understanding outside the narrow range of their professional and business life—some of them, alas, even within such a confined space. In plain terms, this means that teaching has failed to evoke adequate zest for complete living.

In the light of this unquestioned fact we ought to scrutinize assumptions that deny students the quality of being fully alive. Most are subtle, but nonetheless important. For example, in an extraordinarily real sense any deterministic doctrine is a limitation upon the quality of life. That remains true whether it be economic or geopolitical determinism or philosophical positivism or religious predestination or any other concept which has the effect of diminishing man's freedom to master and alter his environment, which reduces his range of choice among an infinite variety, which deprecates the idea that he can make up his own mind and establish his own pattern of values. Behavioristic psychology in its early and crude forms, then in later misunderstandings and misapplications, often tended to reduce man to a mere mechanism which responded to stimuli as a motor to electric impulses.

Certain social philosophies accentuate the tendency to narrow the outlook upon life. Though Aristotle long ago described man as a social being, much current educational discussion would lead to the belief that the discovery was made in our own generation. In a reaction from what appeared as excessive individualism, the pendulum has swung so far in the other direction that students are sometimes thought of as "social units."

For example, the report of the President's Commission on Higher Education[2] said, "The development of social technology is an imperative today." Another contemporary favorite is "social engineering." Reflection will reveal grave connotations in those words. Free will cannot be "engineered"; it is unpredictable and incalculable. It is not possible to "engineer" freedom, which is precisely the right to follow one's own bent. Mechanistic concepts deal with individuals, not as persons of infinite worth,

---

[2] Washington, 1947.

but as social units—a very different matter indeed. Social engineering measures success coldly in operating efficiency rather than in an increase in freedom, happiness, and dignity. The concept of social technology is hostile to the true aims of higher education, for technology is adapted to machines, not to humans. Contrast these doctrines with Jefferson's statement that the University of Virginia was to be "based on the illimitable freedom of the human mind."

All limiting and negative ideas have marked effects upon educational philosophy and practice; all contravene the basic doctrine that the student is alive. Far too much of what passes for "education" assumes that his reflexes must be conditioned, his responses determined, and his patterns set. It is hoped that after he leaves school he will follow along in the fixations which have been predetermined by "specialists" whose own perspective, in many cases, stands in need of correction.

Fixation is the opposite of freedom; it offers no thrilling "brave new world." Conditioned response is the negation of lively imagination and curbs the creative power of the mind. We have no right to denounce the Communists for their dialectic materialism and their totalitarianism if we do not continually expand the aliveness of students and thus enlarge both their true liberty and their capacity for the pursuit of happiness.

Tests and measurements are extremely valuable, but faulty construction to some extent and inept interpretation to a large extent have led to a tragic underestimation of what students can or will do. Unhappily educators have been more impressed by the lower end of the scale than the upper; as a consequence they expect too little of students. Higher education, whose direct obligation does not extend to the lower brackets, should never have fallen into such an egregious error.

Nothing else, however, can explain the prevalent custom of stuffing students with inert information. Such a practice is clear evidence of doubt of the fundamental truth that students are alive. In the process too many facts are "merely received into the mind without being utilized, or tested, or thrown into fresh combinations." A Scotch philosopher well defined such inert materials of instruction: "They are things that don't give you the feeling of aliveness and interest, that don't pull you together and brace you up and make you feel that here is something worth while, something that makes life good and vivid."[3]

It is lack of faith in the aliveness of students, also, that leads to overaccent on vocation, to excessive emphasis upon mere training, to an everlasting routine which desensitizes young people instead of making them more alert. To have laid so much emphasis upon preparation for unchanging vocations under the realities of our time passes all comprehension. Training for a specific job is better adapted to an age long gone, when a man was born into an established pattern and had to follow that rigid design until death. He lived under authoritarian religion, and under the tabus of tradition, inhibited in a thousand ways from which modern man may escape. Under those older circumstances masses of men descended to the plane of automatons, incapable of controlling the politics of their nation; each was a mere unit in society who could not become dominant in its structure or its alteration.

[3] John Macmurray, *Freedom in the Modern World*, London, 1932.

There is something positively absurd about the ultra-vocationalism which neglects the new potentialities of life. In many senses, man is capable of being an individual today as never before in history. Because of the swift miracles of science, communication, and transportation, his capacity for experience is infinitely broadened. The slaves of the lamp and the motor vastly extend his powers. Telegraph, telephone, radio, and greatly improved communication put him in instant touch with all the earth. When the sailing ship gave way to the steamboat and, again, when the airplane came, life took on a new dimension. Now it is simple for a man to travel around the world—an expansion of life in space which was inconceivable even a few years ago.

Contrast the position of an American student today with youth in most of Asia. Human life in the Orient often means very little for the reason that it holds very little. Born to abject poverty with no prospect of rising above the margin of subsistence, tied to the land with no hope of escape, equipped with no ideas except those which were inherited, a person has, as we say, "little to live for." Such a man does not cling to life with the tenacity of those who are privileged to see its potentialities; in the struggle for survival others wipe out his life with callousness. In America, however, we may find life zestful and rich; we may deal with it in broader and more significant terms than those who have not had the opportunities for intellectual development, social mobility, and spiritual growth, and all the other advantages which have been opened to us.

For these reasons it is especially tragic that so much of our education should be dominated by techniques, that students should be indoctrinated, that they should be trained in skills alone, that men should be dealt with substantially as if they were machines. When these things are done, is it any wonder that devotees of cybernetics sometimes ascribe to servomechanisms purposeful behavior and other qualities which heretofore have been regarded as the exclusive possession of living creatures? Should we be surprised that so much stress is laid upon how much more accurate, how much more dependable, how much better than human are the "memories" of electronic monsters? The emphasis should be reversed in order to point out how clever are the men who create them, and build into them such extraordinarily lifelike qualities that the machines seem more alive than many products of an education which fails to remember at every step of the way that "the students are alive."

Even more extraordinary than the failure of teachers to realize that students are alive is the failure of undergraduates fully to appreciate what it means to be alive. Anyone who has helped with their course elections knows how frequently negative factors are dominant. The time of day at which the class meets, the question whether it has a Saturday session, the "personality" of the professor, superficially observed—these trivial straws easily divert a sluggish intellectual stream. Too often choices made with more serious consideration are defensive in character. Children of a generation awed by depression seek a false vocational security. Their questions are economically oriented: What good is it? What will it get me? To what use can I put it?

We speak of an analgesic for relief of pain as "deadening"; the medication is intended to limit sensibility. Vocational overconcentration deadens many aspects of life and has the effect of cutting down awareness of other values. In an effort to become "expert" in one field many students restrict their zones of sensitivity to such an extent as not to participate in the rest of life to the limit of their potentialities. The man or woman who gains vast technical proficiency at the cost of spiritual dullness, esthetic blindness, or ethical insensitivity is not fully alive. In a calculated way he is reducing himself toward the level of a mechanism.

Suicide can be defined as war within one's self to the death. It occurs when a person's life has become so disorganized that, instead of tensions being compensated, they mount to an unbearable point. We all recognize that as a supreme human tragedy. But we do not recognize how tragic is partial suicide, which occurs when a person limits the variety that gives meaning to his life and impairs its innate characteristic—capacity for growth. Anyone who does not strive to develop all his powers—physical, mental, spiritual, and esthetic—has, to the extent that he neglects so to do, failed to remember that he is alive.

On the other hand, as a person broadens his field of attention and alerts his mind in various ways, he widens the frame of reference of a favorite word of those who oppose breadth: relevance. When a new subject, outside a narrow specialty, is suggested, the question is often raised, "What is its relevance?" To a man who sees no reason to study history, the life of people in a far-off country and in a time long past seems dull and unimportant. One whose interests have expanded beyond the narrow range of his own experience finds deep significance in what has happened elsewhere and at earlier times. He comes to see how like our times other eras have been in many respects and how men behaved in comparable circumstances.

We would pity a man with no memory. He would

daily be discovering what ought to be obvious; he would puzzle his wits over things which should be done from mere habit without, as we say, "giving it a thought." In modern society he would be helpless. Similarly, a man with no memory but of his own experience has a very limited basis for action. Unfamiliar with the forces that shaped the problems with which he has to deal, his approach is too naïve. Only through supplementing memory by vicariously entering into the experiences of others can a person reduce the number of baffling situations in which he finds himself.

Memory, lengthened sufficiently by knowledge of earlier experience, supplies at least an analogue to almost every intellectual, moral, social, and political dilemma which confronts us. Life's potential has been infinitely extended by the resources of historical scholarship. It reveals the experiences of ancient times; it clarifies the ways in which earlier people dealt with problems still insistent today, especially those of the ethical and moral life and the relationship of the citizen to politics. In convenient form we have readily at hand not only our own accumulated knowledge, but that of many who have preceded us. We do not have to grope our way blindly through unfamiliar circumstances, but can chart a course by what we know others did, whether rightly or wrongly, in comparable circumstances.

Failure to use memory so expanded as an intellectual tool needlessly hampers our work. There would be no sense whatever in insisting upon using a bent stick, which we might fashion for ourselves as a plow, when we can take advantage of modern gang plows drawn by tractors. There would be no sense in harvesting with a sickle, when there are available reapers and binders to do the work of many men—faster, better, and cheaper. Why, then, should we not utilize to the full the tools of the intellect which are put in our hands through the experience of others? Yet a great deal of education spurns them. It treats as novel what is really shopworn; it misunderstands issues that are before us; it leads to false expectations with regard to peace and war.

Everyone who is fully alive—intellectually, emotionally, spiritually—finds the world so entrancing, life's adventure so thrilling, that his curiosity is insatiable. To him nothing seems wholly foreign; practically everything gains "relevance." Instead of constantly rejecting subjects on the ground that they do not hold any personal appeal, charm is found in more and more ideas. By reflection they are formed into a coherent pattern within the mind. Such comprehensive knowledge helps to banish fear. The wider one makes his area of informed interest, the more competent he is to meet what must be faced with courage and clarity of mind.

There is no reason to restrict the concept that students are alive to the physical and intellectual life; indeed, to do so would be a tragic mistake. The emotions are as capable of cultivation as are mind and body. The necessity for vigorous discipline of the emotions has been explained by the same Scotch philosopher whom I quoted earlier: "Unless the emotions and the intellect are in harmony, rational action will be paralysed" because "a merely intellectual force is powerless against an emotional resistance." He points out that whereas in the modern world there has been an enormous growth of knowledge, there has "been no corresponding emotional development. As a result we are intellectually civilized and emotionally primitive; and we have reached the point at which the development of knowledge threatens to destroy us. Knowledge is power, but emotion is the master of our values and of the uses, therefore, to which we put our power."[4]

Emotion brings us news as significant, truth as valid, and experience as real as any revealed by the intellect. Indeed, the highest emotion of all, love, is the foundation for the religion to which most of us adhere. All the forces which drive us are emotional in character even though the intellect supplies the light and power.

Harmony of intellect, emotion, and physical well-being makes life a great adventure. Disharmony results in undue tension, and our time has been called not so much the atomic era as the age of the barbiturates. American hustle, the competitive spirit, the pressure of the hucksters and others, have induced restlessness that has added to emotional ill-discipline. Neuroses do not arise so much from excessive work as from disharmony and disorganization.

Conscious of unhealthy tension, men seek avenues of escape. Escape from what? Escape from reality—that is, escape from living. So men bore themselves with the incredible inanities of movies, radio, and television, or turn to adventure stories or murder mysteries. Others take to alcohol or narcotics, seeking oblivion.

There are available compensatory activities which are not escapist. They serve to expand life instead of encouraging us to run away from it. There is room—indeed, there is need—for the constant refreshment of one's sense of humor. It is essential to proper perspective; and

---

[4] Macmurray, *op. cit.*

it is not only legitimate, it is wise, to take time for its cultivation.

There are many forms of recreation—physical and mental—which promote sound health and which help in the attainment of that reasonable sense of proportion which the Greeks established as the ultimate good. Among these is literature, through which it is possible to enter into the imaginatively created experience of others and thus broaden perceptions of the meaning of life and savor its great adventure. Joseph Conrad set down his purpose; it was "by the power of the written word to make you hear, to make you feel . . . before all to make you *see*. . . . If I succeed, you shall find there according to your deserts: encouragement, consolation, fear, charm —all you demand—and, perhaps, also that glimpse of truth for which you have forgotten to ask."[5]

Poetry has a place all its own; as it becomes a familiar companion its deepest values emerge. Then its capacity to unite thought and feeling with cadence and rhythm gives it a distinctive quality. The greatest poets seem "to annihilate both time and distance" so that the absorbed reader may enter into other people's stream of life and inhabit far away places as naturally as one goes home.

Music is a form of enrichment. The first time one hears a great composition it may seem a mere jumble of sounds. Regarding a sonata, Marcel Proust wrote: "Often one listens and hears nothing, if it is a piece of music at all complicated to which one is listening the first time. And yet when, later on, this sonata had been played over to me two or three times I found that I knew it quite

---

[5] Cited in Elizabeth Drew, *The Enjoyment of Literature,* New York, 1935.

well. . . . Probably what is wanting, the first time, is not comprehension but memory. For our memory, compared to the complexity of the impression which it has to face while we are listening, is infinitesimal. . . . Of these multiple impressions our memory is not capable of furnishing us with an immediate picture. But that picture gradually takes shape. . . . Great works of art do not begin by giving us all their best."[6] After the ear has been trained and the mind has been schooled to appreciate what is heard, when one has become emotionally sophisticated as well as perceptive, music brings profound satisfaction.

Or looking at the fine arts may so stir one to esthetic awareness that thereafter all beauty has more significance. Whitehead once declared, "Art has a curative function in human experience when it reveals, as in a flash, intimate, absolute Truth regarding the Nature of Things."[7] So art, like music, speaks an international language and has a timeless quality.

None of these things needs to be passively received; one may undertake, as an amateur, to write, to paint, to play, or to compose. Such efforts sharpen the outlook upon the work of others and add richness to appreciation. Any fresh and diverting physical, intellectual, or emotional activity can withdraw a person's attention from his labors and cares; he can relax without deadening his experience, but by deepening and enriching it.

For human beings creative opportunities are almost infinite in variety. Every idea is an invention, if it is really an idea and not a mere parroting of someone else's thought. Each time the imagination evokes an image capable of realization by whatever skill, it is an act of creation, a manifestation of life. Creative power does not

---
[6] *Within a Budding Grove,* New York, 1928.
[7] *Adventures of Ideas,* New York, 1933.

stem from skill; its origin is in imagination, which itself is capable of disciplined development. Of course it requires skill to translate what the mind has conceived, but skill without imagination is sterile.

In an electronic calculator an idea is only a datum—cold, hard, nonmalleable—to be "stored" in an appropriate tube against the time when it is summoned. But if the student and the idea are both alive, their interaction one upon the other is a unique occurrence in the history of the world. For no two living people were ever alike and no two ever responded to the same idea in precisely the same way; the possibilities therefore are, in the most literal sense of the word, infinite.

It is the balance of profession, avocation, political action, social life, cultural and religious interest that makes a free man fully know, and value, his freedom. It never is safe to short-circuit any phase of life, and it is tragic when the wellsprings of interest—of aliveness—are left to dry up.

To what conclusion does this reasoning lead? America proclaimed a revolutionary doctrine: all men have an equal right to life, liberty, and the pursuit of happiness. That faith shaped the course of our history and fired the imagination of the oppressed abroad. It gave us moral leadership in the struggle for freedom.

After the First World War disillusionment and economic depression combined to drain away the passionate confidence which had marked our faith. The initiative passed to the totalitarians; and during the last quarter century the rights of men were curbed rather than expanded. After the defeat of Fascism and Nazism, Communism alone challenged democracy. That challenge has not yet been met.

Industrial energy revived before moral and political confidence returned. The United States led the world in a technological revolution of amazing proportions. The productivity of our economy upset the historic balance of the world. It furnished support for war-weakened nations and inspired them with fresh hope. At the same time its dominant size awakened fears lest instability here carry all the free world down in another crash like that of two decades ago.

From those doubts and fears we must escape. The United States must recapture the intellectual and moral initiative in the struggle for "a brave new world." Without that mere "situations of strength" will prove sterile. In that recovery higher education, in the true meaning of the term, has a vital role.

We must make available to every competent American not only training in skills and a growing mastery over nature. In addition to those essentials, we must cultivate far more intensively the disciplines of the humanities and the social studies. By their help we may attain our fullest potentialities as men. That is the only path to leadership in the world's quest for peace and freedom. The future security of the nation rests with students who are alive.

V ∽ Cultural Affairs and Foreign Relations

EDUCATIONAL administration in the United States is quite different from that profession in the rest of the world. The reasons are historical and need not concern us, but one function of an American administrator is to search for money. Some months ago, while I was engaged in that task, the prospective donor turned a cold eye upon me and asked: "Why are you going to Kuala Lumpur? Is this not The *American* Assembly?" What I have to say is my answer to those two questions. It was not all said on the spur of the moment; yet the spontaneous response differed in no important respect from this reflective elaboration.

One brief sentence in Langdon Warner's *The Enduring Art of Japan*[1] epitomizes the significance of cultural affairs in international relations. There can be "no progress for us, no improvement, no originality, without deliberate study of the stream of the spirit through the entire human race." He might well have said, also, that without such devoted attention there can be no peace.

Asian-American Assembly, Kuala Lumpur, Malaya, April 11, 1963.

[1] Cambridge (Mass.), 1952.

Warner's statement offers adequate explanation of this Assembly; indeed, it indicates why it is essential to have international gatherings—many of them. Like other profound truths, the quotation has a deceptive simplicity. But the inferences to be drawn from it are subtle and complex.

We know that always and everywhere there has been a quest for an understanding of life and death, and a common yearning for the infinite. Myths and traditions, religious rites and festivals are common to all peoples throughout history. Even in civilizations long out of touch with the rest of the world, like the Aztecs of Mexico and the Incas of Peru, the priesthood was a large and important group. Throughout the ages the importance of religious feeling appears in impressive structures whenever men knew how to build them. Indeed, they were often the most striking manifestations of architecture, engineering, and artisanship. At one time and place, the impulse took the form of a pyramid; at another, the Parthenon; during the Middle Ages, a Gothic cathedral; in still another age or area, a stupa, a temple; all reflect the stream of the human spirit.

Survivals from long before recorded history—such as paintings in French and Spanish caves—furnish reminders that in all times and in all places the urge to self-expression has produced art in many forms—painting, sculpture, architecture, and artifacts of infinite variety. Music likewise represents a universal impulse; tonal scales, rhythms, instruments vary, yet all have important common elements.

It is a stark fact of history that there has been both a conscious, and perhaps a more disastrous unconscious, failure to appreciate manifestations of the stream of the spirit in other peoples and in other parts of the world. The purposeful policy of cultural isolation is typified by the long effort of Japan to shut itself off from outside influences. That instance is far from unique; I select it merely because it is familiar and was facilitated by the island character of the geography.

The effort was indicative of a passion, observable in many other instances, to preserve a cultural individuality, unalloyed with alien elements. In some instances the determination survived for centuries—a reminder that historically there have been powerful currents and eddies within the stream of the spirit. Nonetheless, even the distinctive individuality which a culture sought to preserve without contamination had itself been shaped, to a large extent, by prior, perhaps forgotten, contacts with others. Total isolation has never been attained.

For my generation in the United States, cultural isolation was quite unconscious. It stemmed partly from geography, for we were separated from Europe and Asia by two great oceans. It was stimulated by political considerations—a long and powerful tradition of non-alignment and non-involvement. It was further reinforced by preoccupation with the immense tasks of conquering a continental wilderness; this proved so engrossing as almost to blot out awareness of faraway lands. As a result of all these factors, the history of Asia was a blank page in the schooling of my generation and of those who had gone before.

Insofar as we were taught cultural values, they were strictly European; systematic exposure even to them was meager. The classical tradition dominated education and most of us knew more of Greek and Roman civilization than of modern cultural life. So far as formal instruction was concerned, therefore, culture belonged to the ancient world. Opportunities for personal participation in cultural activities were few in most American communities, for the nation was still largely a pioneer, and dominantly a rural, society.

Both these examples of cultural isolation—Japan and the United States—had some physical basis. Even more tragic are the instances where there was no such geographical basis. Instead, two cultures lived together physically but remained infinitely far apart spiritually. That is part of the desperate tragedy of slavery in the United States—with all the residues of misunderstanding and maladjustment that persist even a century after slavery was outlawed. That, also, is the worst inheritance of colonialism. A leading writer on Latin America expressed well the effects of colonialism on that continent: the natives existed as "a nation within a nation, a culture within a culture"; they and their conquerors were "two peoples living in proximity but belonging to two different universes." This spiritual isolation is now, perforce, giving way, but the change proceeds in an atmosphere of bitterness which hinders the fresh start that most former colonial powers would like to make.

Whatever the occasion for the failure to appreciate other cultures, the inevitable consequence has always and everywhere been a blighting parochialism. One African leader summed up the problem of his nation with rare candor: "It is not easy to achieve in one's own heart and mind the peaceful coexistence of traditional and modern elements. And yet without such peaceful coexistence no new and original African personality will be able to emerge."

It is from the withering effects of isolation that all—East and West—must now make a determined effort to escape. Over hundreds of years, multifold ignorances have so deepened and intensified that it requires an extraordinary effort, not only of the mind but of the will, to modify political, social, and cultural traditions, in order to do even what we have come to recognize as profoundly necessary.

Those of us who come to Asia from the United States, therefore, are here on no mission of mere curiosity, to see and hear strange and exotic things. Nor do we come bearing gifts; The American Assembly is no part of any kind of aid program, either public or private, economic or cultural. We come as part of a mutual endeavor to heighten awareness that the stream of the spirit does indeed unite the whole human race.

The Assembly is dedicated to the realization that in an age overly impressed with size, numbers, wealth, and power as determinants of policy, culture should supply one of its more stable elements, just as it gives richness and balance to private life. Policy-makers have sadly neglected culture because it is not a pliable instrument, subject to easy manipulation or the achievement of momentary advantage. Indeed, in the short run, cultural contacts are likely to produce unexpected and disturbing consequences rather than some calculated result.

On the other hand, cultural roots run so deep, and their growth is so tough, that geography, economic force, and military might can all be defied. This is illustrated in the Western Hemisphere by the influence of the Iberian peninsula upon Central and South America. Spain and Portugal are far away across a great ocean; they lost all political control well over a century ago; their contribution to the economic life of Latin America does not compare with that of the United States or several other nations; neither Iberian nation is in any position to aid in defense of the area; their contribution to governmental practice is in the far past and was never conspicuously helpful. Nevertheless, cultural bonds remain so strong that all these handicaps to influence are, to a significant degree, offset.

Other illustrations of the strength of cultural forces abound. Even the last World War, which many falsely described as "total," impaired but could not destroy cultural continuity. Shakespeare remained a favorite dramatist among Germans, and German music still dominated American orchestral repertoires.

Art continued to play its great role; the language of beauty remained as accessible to foe as to friend and required no interpreter, no mediator. It represented something so deep within the human spirit that it could defy censorship and all other forms of political authority. Once again, as many times before in history, it was demonstrated that no external power can inhibit the memory or suborn the imagination.

Moreover, learned publications, particularly in science, were exchanged among "enemies" with the connivance of their governments. Later, when the reversal of alliances produced the "cold war," cultural exchanges were warmly received on both sides, even during the most frigid political periods.

In the United States it has been a fundamental part of our tradition that educational and cultural activities should be left to private initiative. Even when they are publicly supported, they have been the responsibility of state and local authorities. Nevertheless, recognition of the reality and significance of cultural forces in international life has now led to the appointment of an Assistant Secretary of State for educational and cultural affairs. We can hope that this venture implies no rosy expectations that it will have a rapid, direct, or heavy impact on international relations. If the Congress were to demand quick, provable "results" or if the new division were to attempt some superficial "demonstration" of its value, its purpose would be defeated. Its true function is modestly to symbolize—and reinforce—the effort to appreciate the oneness of the human spirit, everywhere.

If culture is not to be measured by tangibles, it follows that the size, or power, or economic resources of a nation are almost—and may be wholly—irrelevant to its cultural significance. Even by the standards of the ancient world, Periclean Athens constituted a tiny fragment of the earth's surface; its population was not great. Size proved to be no detriment to the cultural impact of that ancient city-state, which was both profound and permanent.

That illustration is a reminder that taste, skill, and wisdom have never been distributed in proportion to area or population; they are even less closely related to wealth or power. Cultural riches exist quite apart from natural resources, industrial development, fiscal magnitude, or military might. This Assembly is a kind of demonstration of the sincerity of that belief and of its deep significance for international intercourse.

Nevertheless, it must be conceded that, historically, within each society status and wealth have had some effects. This is revealed by the fact that in most of the world culture existed on two levels. There was a culture of the elite—the court, the nobles, the wealthy, the learned. Simultaneously there flourished a folk culture which has been described as "of no less intrinsic beauty and perhaps of even greater vitality and significance" expressed in structures and artifacts "all made by means of a traditional and instinctive technique, by people who could count but not calculate and draw but not write."[2] Clearly this double level shows that social structure directly affected cultural life.

I recall when this coexistence of two cultural levels was borne in upon my consciousness with great force. On a visit to Stockholm I attended a folk dance competition in the Royal Opera House. The teams of contestants came from more than twenty countries. Their costumes showed great variety in design and coloring, but there was a fundamental similarity in their dances. The next week a ballet company appeared on the same stage. The first set of dances had been simple and vigorous, in some instances to the point of being acrobatic; the second was stylized, complicated, and symbolic, though also demanding strength, agility, and grace. The folk dancers were the product of the countryside; in origin the ballet belonged to the court.

A second significant reality was also dramatically brought to mind on that same occasion: there are fundamental similarities in folk expression not only in many countries, but on separate continents. This is true even when there has been no significant contact since recorded history began. For example, some of the tribal dances in Africa and among American Indians have marked similarities. The rhythms and the musical accompaniments have noticeable likenesses. With a change of paint

---

[2] Warner, *op. cit.*

on their bodies and some alteration of costume and a reshaping of musical instruments one might be mistaken for the other except by an anthropologist. In the same way, there are striking resemblances in textile patterns and other art forms among people from many parts of the world. The stream of the spirit has somehow found common expression even without known physical contact.

This Assembly also calls attention to the undoubted reality that the United States has made some distinctive contributions. Specifically, in cultural life, as in political, social, and economic aspects of experience, America represented revolutionary doctrine. The Declaration of Independence contains five key words: "all men are created equal." If all the rest of that famous manifesto had been lost, and those five words survived, they would still have had a profound impact upon the world. They constituted an astounding assertion in 1776, challenging all previous social and political experience. Their boldness was the more dramatic since the challenge came from a sparsely populated, straggling string of undeveloped colonies, scattered along a coastline with a wilderness crowding behind them, in a remote part of the world.

When the five key words were written there was slavery in America; there were social classes in most countries and rigid castes in others. Nearly everywhere privilege was inherited by a favored few as though it were a physical possession; for all others the lack of privilege was a fact of life, to be accepted along with such other unpleasant realities as death and taxes.

To appreciate the thrust of those five words, it must be emphasized that they were not a rhetorician's polished phrase, or anything exclusively Jeffersonian. It was said that in drafting them Jefferson "plagiarized the atmosphere." Moreover, John Adams, a rival of Jefferson, said they were "intended to be an expression of the American mind." So they have remained, as is shown in the poetry of the late Robert Frost. A leading critic said his verse came "as close to defining America as any man's poetry has done." In his last volume these lines occur:[3]

> Had but Columbus known enough
> . . . .
> He had been given to behold
> The race's future trial place,
> A fresh start for the human race.

There was no trace of chauvinism and no bombast whatever in Frost; he was seeking to stress the revolutionary spirit embodied in the words "all men are created equal." It was a theme to which his poetry returned again and again.

The present enormous size and strength of the United States add nothing to either the challenge or the potency of the words themselves. During the century and three quarters between 1776 and 1963 there have been vast changes all around the world. Nonetheless, the pronouncement remains almost as astonishing today as when the words were written.

Like all great affirmations of faith, the assertion was cast in the form of an absolute; it was called "self-evident," as though it were an axiom, requiring no proof. Yet, since it was not a description of the actual situation anywhere in the world, it was more in the nature of proph-

---

[3] From "America Is Hard to See," a much longer poem, from *In the Clearing* by Robert Frost. Copyright 1951, © 1962 by Robert Frost. Reprinted by permission of Holt, Rinehart and Winston, Inc.

ecy. There was then no anthropological or other scientific basis for the new article of faith. It calls to mind part of the title of the last poem written by Frost: "The prophets really prophesy as mystics." The realists of that day might well have said that the authors of these words were seeing visions and dreaming dreams.

Most of us are familiar enough with the fact that so absolute a dogma of equality, stated as part of a fundamental national purpose, was unique in the political and social and economic world. We seldom pause to reflect that it was equally unique in the cultural world. Until very modern times, what had been true in Periclean Athens, where the cultured were a small fraction of the population, was true to a greater or lesser degree around the world. Everywhere high culture and in most places even folk culture were the possession of tiny minorities of all the people. This fact passed unremarked as though it had been ordained from the beginning of the world.

In the United States, by slow stages, but with accelerating pace, the spirit of equality became so strong that there arose a determination that no individual should be denied the fulfillment of his highest potential. In politics the aim was embodied in virtually universal suffrage; it was symbolized in the tradition of advance from birth in a log cabin to the presidency in the White House. In economic life it found outlet in progress from rags to riches in one generation. In cultural life it denied any limitations whatever upon the pursuit of any art or calling.

That spirit accounts for the enormous stress put upon universal free education. It stemmed directly from these five words: "all men are created equal." What a sharp break that was with the previous history of America itself is shown in the contrast between two statements made approximately a century apart.

A royal governor of Virginia had said in 1671: "I thank God we have no free schools nor printing. . . . For learning has brought disobedience and heresy and sects into the world; and printing has divulged them and libels against the government. God keep us from both."

The other statement was made by another governor of Virginia, Thomas Jefferson. He maintained that "if a nation expects to be ignorant and free, it expects what never was and never will be." Far from regretting printing, he went so far as to assert: "Were it left me to decide whether we should have a government without newspapers, or newspapers without a government, I should not hesitate a moment to prefer the latter."

These words were indicative of a passion for bringing culture to everyone. To that end the education which was to be available to all was not merely elementary schooling. Every student was to carry his intellectual development as far as his ambition and his ability would permit and at the bare minimum of cost to him or his family. This produced a unique educational event in history. As the pioneers pushed westward they planted colleges as soon as they developed settlements.

In 1862 the federal government gave a great thrust to the movement by a subsidy consisting of grants of land. This process resulted in a profusion of institutions of varying quality. They did not wholly break with the old world tradition but they did modify it to meet pioneer and frontier conditions. They had a special function—to help mold a polyglot collection of people drawn from many countries into one nation able to meet the responsibilities of democracy.

I remember when, as an undergraduate in a classical

course, I joined fellow students in scorn of these colleges because they stressed agriculture and engineering. As undergraduates are apt to be, we were too hasty. Those institutions met the special needs of their time and place; they represented democracy on the march.

Now, more than a half century later, many have grown into mature universities with high standards, educating —at little expense to the students—a vast host of young people. They carry on fundamenal research with great competence and maintain medical schools of highest quality. Many have outstanding music and art departments; several make genuine contributions to the theater. They are characterized by brilliant achievements in the humanities. In short, they exhibit a range, a vitality, and a competence no less than astonishing.

Others among the pioneer institutions have become independent four-year colleges of arts and sciences—characteristically American institutions—often with standards, within their limited fields, equal to the best universities. This vast and varied educational system played a vital part in creating a truly democratic culture.

It would be difficult to conceive of a more perfect embodiment of the passion for individual development in an atmosphere of complete freedom, really justifying Jefferson's hopes. Of course such sweeping objectives could not be attained in one giant stride. Nor did the founders of the nation expect their dreams to become reality in the twinkling of an eye. Still, they would be astonished at the maturity of the cultural revolution they so boldly inaugurated.

Perfectibility remains beyond reach, but unflagging zeal for the ideal leads social critics to highlight every deficiency in its full realization. They are shrill in denouncing what seems to their eager spirits slowness of progress. They forget that the five words of the Declaration of Independence had a somewhat utopian character. As the goal is approached, it is refined and made more profound. What would have been accepted as satisfactory in one generation seems like crudity to the next. This explains the vast ferment of self-criticism which deplores every imperfection in fields political, economic, educational, and cultural.

The historian would say that the impatient critics are wrong, that progress has been faster than could reasonably have been expected. He would emphasize that within a century of the proclamation ending slavery many Negroes have already come to occupy high places in government, are conspicuous in musical life, have attained a significant influence in education and in letters, have won remarkable positions in the entertainment world, and are notable in athletics. Progress from the status of a human chattel to the position of a respected figure within a century is a tremendous acceleration of earlier historical experience. It should be said that since the end of the colonial period the same phenomenon is to be observed in Brazil, Cuba, Venezuela, and Panama.

The social critic responds that what the record shows even more clearly is the tragedy of previous intentional impoverishment of our cultural life. Though so much talent has been rapidly revealed, the critic insists we have only scratched the surface of the vast mine of abilities wasted for centuries and even now but meagerly exploited. He demands genuine personal fulfillment for all and fresh energy in the search for talents still hidden.

The insistence upon the equality of men led to a determination to involve all the people and weld together the two levels of culture, uniting the art of the elite and folk art. It has been well said that "the proverbial wisdom of the peasant and the sophisticated knowledge of the elite operate on two different planes and it is difficult for them to meet." It is even more difficult to merge them; nonetheless the effort is afoot.

Amid profound social changes we can sometimes observe the process in the life of a single individual. Nearly fifty years ago I first heard Carl Sandburg when he moved from college to college singing folk songs and reciting his own verses. Now he is recognized as a notable historian, author of a monumental life of Lincoln, a literary figure, a distinguished poet. He dramatically unites both types of culture.

Democratization of the arts and the fusing of the two cultures appears in the characteristic American development of the musical operetta. In "Oklahoma!," in "West Side Story," and in many other immensely popular musical plays, the ballet has been brought into the theater but modified by the folk tradition. Nearly all agree that the union has enriched an art which might have become stylized to the point of sterility.

This same attempt to bridge the two levels of culture and democratize the result is shown in the enormous popularity of Negro spirituals. The mood they evoke came to dominate some of the most successful Broadway plays, such as "Green Pastures" and "Porgy and Bess." American jazz, born of Negro rhythms, has gone around the world.

In an effort to give historical as well as philosophical justification for this democratic union of the cultures, men have searched for evidences that once there was an egalitarian society and a common culture before stratification set in and hierarchies became established. Such efforts have produced some sentimentalization of folk art as in some respects superior to high culture. Folk art, says a prominent author, is "immune from the diseases of snobbery, plutocracy, and the cults" and usually corresponds to "the three transcendentals—the good, the true, and the beautiful."

Despite such occasional excesses of enthusiasm, the egalitarian passion represents a genuine conviction that riches of the spirit and wealth of talent are distributed around the world without distinction of race, creed, or politics. Opportunity for cultural life is no longer to be determined on the one hand by rank and status, or on the other by wealth or power.

I come to a final question: Why is it so difficult to do what we know must be done, and what in our hearts we wish to do? In many ways the attainment of our objective should be easier than ever before. Contacts, once difficult to the point of impossibility, are now easy. One can come here to Malaya from the eastern shores of the United States in less than two days. That epitomizes a revolution in ease of meeting produced by the explosion of knowledge in science and technology. All forms of communication—radio, television, films, mass publications—have burgeoned to an extent inconceivable even to the last generation. Trade and commerce have become world-wide; no nation now lives in economic isolation. Security also has become a global problem; weapons no longer discriminate between combatant and non-combatant. Even if the initial explosion is escaped, the lethal poisoning of the atmosphere knows no neutrals.

But it would be foolish to forget that centrifugal forces are also strong. Chief of these is habit; it is embedded far below the surface of consciousness. In his "Ode on

Intimations of Immortality," the poet William Wordsworth wrote of the weight of custom, "deep almost as life."

Abraham Lincoln had profound intuitive insights. He spoke of the agonies that must be endured as expiation for the monstrous sin of slavery. A century after he had put an end to the legal status of the evil we are still paying its penalties. Habit has proved, in Mississippi and elsewhere, "deep almost as life" and postpones the day when we shall be free of the burden of guilt.

Colonialism is all but gone from the free world, but no one should be so naïve as to think that its bitter aftertaste will soon disappear. The old habits endured so long that they became too deeply engrained to be thrown off like a garment.

For these reasons, even with the best will in the world, difficulties were sure to be severe and prolonged. But we cannot shut our eyes to the fact that there are those who think they profit in some way (political or otherwise) by nourishing resentments, by the stimulation of prejudice, by misrepresenting motives, and by indoctrination of hates. Sometimes these disruptive tactics are masked under the cloak of nationalism. Often, indeed, xenophobia is promoted most actively where "the making of a nation has proved more difficult than the proclamation of nationalism as a credo and a policy." In many instances there is no real sense of nationhood, but only a political entity.

This is something Americans should know from their own history. There is a phrase in George Washington's Farewell Address: "if we remain one people." Today when that passage is read it does not stand out. But when it was written it had deep meaning. The first government of the nation had virtually collapsed. The new government was only eight years old and was faced not only with hostile neighbors but with many forms of internal dissension. It took years for a truly national spirit to develop, and even after seventy years of the Union it was challenged by a long and costly civil war.

The making of a nation often tempts leaders, in the effort to stress individuality, deliberately to break ties with other cultures with which they had been associated. Sometimes, it is clear, this is done to achieve political, at the expense of cultural, objectives; often it is part of a search for an identity which has proved elusive.

There are two broad roads to folly. One is to pursue a calculated policy of ignorance regarding the rest of the world in an effort to heighten the sense of selfhood. The other is to move into the never-never land of sentimentality, and repeat "all men are brothers" as a kind of incantation, hoping for the magical effects that pronouncing "open sesame" and rubbing Aladdin's lamp produced in the tales of *The Arabian Nights*.

Instead, we must cultivate what, at an earlier time, I called the subsoil of peace—mutual appreciation of each other's progress in science, in the fine arts, in literature, and every other manifestation of human genius, without nervous reference to national origin. This is an area of competitive coexistence where we need have no fear, for these evidences of the vast riches of the human spirit transcend boundaries and all other indications of the divisiveness of politics.

The true road is shown by Langdon Warner's brief but vital remark. For old nations and new, for East and West, for North and South, progress depends upon "deliberate study of the stream of the spirit through the entire human race."

VI ~ Dawn Will Break: A Point of View on International Affairs

SOMETIMES a book has the power to vivify your own thought. It calls up ideas from the back of your mind and puts them in the spotlight. The last lectures of the great Spanish philosopher-historian, Ortega y Gasset, have been published under a title singularly appropriate for today—*Man and Crisis.*

A date, says Ortega—any date, say this one, December 5, 1958—is apparently precise. Yet its precision is so superficial as to be deceptive. For it does not convey the same meaning to different persons. It is observed not in objective terms alone—the precise element—but subjectively through the lens of experience. A five-year-old knows no history, his experience is limited, his memory is short. To him the date will have a very restricted meaning; he sees it myopically. A man of sixty-five observes the date quite differently. He has read history, his experience is broad, his memory is long; his perspective might be called telescopic—his view of the date is from a different eminence.

Student Conference on United States Affairs, United States Military Academy, West Point, December 5, 1958.

On a specific date, about three weeks ago, I read two statements. One was the first sentence of Ortega's book: "In June of 1633, Galileo Galilei, then seventy years of age, was forced to kneel before the Inquisitorial Tribunal of Rome and renounce the Copernican theory, a concept which was to make possible the modern science of physics."

On the very day I read that passage, I also read that Boris Pasternak, then sixty-eight years old, poet and author of the novel *Dr. Zhivago,* was forced to bow before the majesty of the Kremlin and renounce the Nobel Prize.

To one who had never heard of Galileo, the coincidence of reading the two sentences upon the same day would mean nothing. To one who has learned the meaning of tyranny through study of history, whose own experience encompasses the observation of a succession of tyrannies, whose memory is filled with slaughter by the tyrants—with the liquidation of the Kulaks, the holocaust of the Jews, the murder of Matteotti, the purges of Mao Tse-tung—the coincidence of reading of one act of renunciation on the very day of another somewhat like it, though they were three centuries apart, produced a flood of reflections.

One of those was a fresh appreciation of the fact that, as part of our normal equipment, each of us possesses a mental image of our time. It is a kind of montage in which a succession of events are recorded photographically, superimposed one upon another. All the problems and perils, all the ambitions and achievements, all the dilemmas and defeats make up the total picture. To one man the resultant image will seem clear and sharp; we say "he knows his own mind." To another the image will be blurred and confused and he will move in an aura of frustration.

Inevitably, my montage has a different perspective, a different depth, a different dominance from yours. Consequently, your estimate of the possibilities and probabilities, your idea of appropriate ways and available means to attain desired ends, will differ from mine. If we are to communicate meaningfully, I must make an effort to observe the world, imaginatively, through your eyes. But you cannot be passive; you must make a like but complementary effort to see the world to some extent in the image in which I perceive it. If meaning is to be extracted from a speech, it requires effort on the part of the listener at least as great as that exerted by the speaker—sometimes more, unhappily.

Perhaps we can begin this mutual effort by agreeing to the deceptively simple proposition that, while history is composed of facts, facts do not make history. The facts are real enough; but they are literally beyond the sands of the sea in number, for everything that ever happened to anyone anywhere is the material for history. Within this infinitely large mass of facts, data do not arrange themselves in any meaningful relationship; they are a vast jumble of confused sequences carrying within themselves no indication of cause or effect. By themselves, they make no sense whatever.

History, as we know it, is a construct of the human mind. From out the infinite range of data, some man selects such facts as seem to him at that moment to be capable of being endowed with meaning in the particular context within which his mind is just then moving. This explains the element of truth in the saying that each generation writes its own history. In coping with the present, men reach back into human experiences to find precedents, hints, indications of what succeeded and what failed. As current preoccupations change continually, there is constant search of the past for relevant experience.

In my childhood, I was taught to look upon Britain as *the* enemy. This was because of the manner in which my history books described the Revolutionary War, the tense situation during the War Between the States, rivalry over an Isthmian canal—and other episodes. In your early days, the enemy was Germany, Japan, and then Russia—with Britain as our staunchest ally. If each generation does not entirely rewrite history, the emphasis, the interpretation change from time to time—and sometimes with dramatic swiftness.

The speed of change is facilitated if people make little effort to think for themselves. When, as a teacher, I asked proof of some statement, the frequent response was, "It says so in the book." This tendency to avoid thought leads to a tragic conclusion: masses of men are as ready to believe fiction as to face reality. Indeed, they are ready to die for idols, and literally millions have laid down their lives out of loyalty to ideals which time proved palpably false. If heroism had been displayed only in good causes, the history of the world—and more particularly of the twentieth century—would have been very different from the record as it stands.

You are too young to remember how masses of men —men by tens and hundreds of thousands—gathered and shouted themselves into a frenzy of exaltation while Hitler talked absolute nonsense. Read the turgid inanities of *Mein Kampf* and gasp in amazement that it could be taken as a sane exposition of a program. When one reads today what he said then, it fills one with astonishment that millions—actually millions—were hypnotized into adoration of such a mountebank, whose ideas were so empty, so confused, so vicious.

I recall traveling in Italy at the height of Mussolini's power. Everywhere were posters picturing *il Duce* and bearing the legend, "He will decide." That promise was one of the principal sources of his popularity. To escape the agony of thinking and deciding for themselves men were willing to throw away precious, hard-won rights.

In our country, the great depression of the thirties sharply altered the outlook upon history as past experience. Things said then were repeated often enough to be regarded as gospel—not because of their truth but through mere iteration. They came to be accepted unthinkingly, forming barriers to sound observation and thought thereafter.

One persistent myth was that our forefathers were nurtured in the faith that progress was inevitable; indeed it has been asserted that Americans have traditionally regarded human progress as "automatic." A more inappropriate word could not be found, yet it gained such wide currency as to be accepted as a truism—not subject to challenge.

It was conceded, because it could not be hidden, that they had troubles. But the myth asserted that there was always a rainbow even in the midst of the storm. In consequence—so ran the myth—they faced their problems without the doubts, confusions, and dilemmas which your generation finds so sharp, so painful, so frustrating. This fiction about your forebears was one of those "circumambient convictions" which one absorbs from the environmental atmosphere without thought—a ready-made concept.

As the late Al Smith used to say, "Let us look at the record." We may start with Ralph Waldo Emerson. I choose him not only because his name is familiar to you but also because he is a comfortable time away from us. Despite differences between your age and mine, he clearly ranks as a forefather, both to you and to me. Further, he was a philosopher who found honor in his own country, and in his own day and generation. His credentials as a spokesman are, therefore, well authenticated.

In 1837 appeared this passage in his journal: "Society has played out its last stroke. It is checkmated. Young men have no hope. Adults stand like day laborers, idle in the streets. None calleth us to labor. The present generation is bankrupt of principles and hope, as of property."

Admittedly, that passage was written during an economic depression. That heightens its validity as evidence in our present inquiry. The point at issue is precisely whether in times of stress men of earlier days felt defeated and frustrated, or whether, on the other hand, they were buoyed amid a sea of troubles by an undaunted faith in progress. No one, by any stretch of imagination, would regard that entry as reflecting a serene faith in automatic progress. His words were dramatic: society, he asserted, is checkmated; youth, he declared, are without hope.

Let us take another example, from 1844, after that depression about which Emerson wrote was over. Henry H. Ellsworth, first United States Commissioner of Patents, was a respected and influential figure in his day, a fair choice as a spokesman for thoughtful men. He was aware of progress. "The advancement of the arts, from year to year, taxes our credulity, and seems to presage the arrival of that period when human improvement must end." That has not the hard, bitter pessimism that characterized Emerson's statement some years earlier, but it has no buoyant expectation of a golden age toward which America was marching with confident stride. Indeed, it was seriously suggested that in a few years the patent office should be closed. Gadgets would be developed, a better mousetrap for instance, but the vital inventions would all have been discovered, and it would not be worth while to maintain a government agency to register the trivia that remained to be invented.

The theme that advances could not continue indefinitely recurs again and again. Forty years after Ellsworth's prediction of an end to progress, Carroll D. Wright echoed it. Wright was the first Commissioner in the Bureau of Labor (later the Department of Labor) and the first president of Clark University. He said: "Industry has been enormously developed, cities have been transformed, distances covered, and a new set of economic tools has been given in profusion to rich countries, and in a more reasonable amount to poorer ones. . . . It is true that the discovery of new processes of manufacture will undoubtedly continue . . . but it will not leave room for a marked extension, such as has been witnessed during the last fifty years, or afford a remunerative employment of the vast amount of capital which has been created during that period. The market price . . . will continue low, no matter what the cost of production may be. The day of large profits is probably past.

There may be room for further intensive, but not extensive development of industry in the present area of civilization."[1]

The date deserves stress, for 1886 was in the horse and buggy days. Electric lights were not yet common. Alternating current was regarded as so deadly there was agitation to prohibit it by law and Thomas A. Edison insisted that no companies bearing his name should use other than direct current. It was before telephones, talking machines, movies, automobiles, airplanes, radio, television, atomic power, and nuclear fission. Yet here was an educated leader calling a halt, in his mind, to human progress.

This dim view of future developments continued. It accounted for the fact that the achievement of flight by the Wright brothers at Kitty Hawk got almost no notice in the daily press. The alleged faith in ineluctable progress was not strong enough to give editors—to whom, for want of columnists, we had at that time to look for perpetual wisdom—any vision of what that accomplishment implied.

Come a little closer and look at the view of a man not quite old enough to be your grandfather. In 1932, Stuart Chase wrote: "For the first time in our national history since the opening of the West, we have to deal with a roughly static rather than an expanding structure. There is no prairie, no mountain, no forest to which we can escape; there are no elastic real estate values to muffle the impact of our industrial blunders. Our luck has run out; we have at last to face real things in a real world."[2]

Perhaps you want higher authority—a more authentic

---

[1] United States Documents, Serial 2382, 49 Cong. 1 Sess., House Executive Document 1, Part V. Italics supplied.
[2] *A New Deal,* New York, 1932.

voice. No one can question the credentials of a man four times elected to the presidency of the United States, Franklin D. Roosevelt. Speaking in 1933, when our gross national product was less than half the 450 billion of last year, he said: "It seems to me that our physical economic plant will not expand in its future at the same rate at which it has expanded in the past. We may build more factories, but the fact remains that we have enough to supply all our domestic needs, and more, if they are used." Again he stressed the point: "Our task now is not discovery or exploitation of natural resources or necessarily of producing more goods. It is the soberer, less dramatic business of administering resources and plants already in hand."

I need not pile up quotations for I can give you first-hand testimony. As an undergraduate I had "facts" presented to me that proved to be wrong—not only about economics, politics, society, but even the atom, then defined as the smallest unit of matter, instead of a universe *in parvo*. But let us review some of these alleged facts.

One was that the population of the United States by 1950 would have been stabilized at about 150 million; the birth rate was declining, immigration was being choked off, and we were headed for a population plateau. This was proved statistically; population trends had been charted; the curve had been determined by extrapolation; thus by this modern method of authentic prophecy truth had been revealed. We were told as "fact" that the population of France was in decline and would continue to decline, and that its loss of stature as a great power would be occasioned by this continuous and irreversible shrinkage of its population.

I was told that by 1950 our coal resources would be

exhausted; we would face a shortage of power because water power could not supply our needs and coal could no longer supply our necessities. It was clear to the learned professor who was stuffing me with this nonsense that by 1950 our oil supply would also be used up. Natural gas had not been commercially developed and was not regarded seriously as an asset. The atom had not yet been mentioned as a source of energy. You may think that it just happened that I had a fool for a professor. On the contrary, when he had completed my miseducation, he subsequently held appointments in two of the famous universities of the country.

These "facts" which were taught me with such conviction are not one whit more unreal than many of the "truths" transmitted to you. Even within the last decade you have been told that the world resources of uranium would be exhausted in a very few years; yet the other day I heard experts using an idiom which is strictly modern —we now have so much uranium that it is "running out of our ears," which I take it means a plenitude.

Old fashioned orators had a figure of speech drawn from their classical studies. When they wanted to intimate that a speaker was engaging in superfluity, they would ask: Must he pile Pelion on Ossa? I do not want to put mountains of evidence on top of one another, though it would be possible to do so until it was abundantly evident that the allegation of faith in automatic progress is a product of a misinterpretation of history, not a true picture of the faith of our fathers. This is not to say that optimism has been lacking. To make any such assertion would be as bad a caricature of the past as the one I am criticizing.

It just happens that I was born in the year that the

United States government announced officially that the frontier was closed. Many regarded that announcement as the end of the era of opportunity. It had been an era of opportunity in many senses. My grandfather, my uncle, and one of my cousins each got land by homesteading, by mere occupation and use, without any payment. Yet since the closure of the frontier and the end of the very real opportunities that it did present, the range of opportunities has widened infinitely. That word "infinitely" was chosen with care; it is precise and not extravagant. The era in which you are exercising your powers has seen the opening of frontiers vastly more significant than the unsettled West of America, and vistas of achievement far more challenging.

Once we have destroyed the false notion that our fathers had serene faith in automatic progress, our perspective is fundamentally altered. We are in a position to admit that there is not a trouble spot anywhere in the world that has not long plagued mankind with its problems.

Palestine—the Middle East—is seething. It helps to remember that the name Armageddon—Biblical symbol of the ultimate conflict—comes from that area. It was known in antiquity. It became part of the title of a British general in the First World War, Lord Allenby of Megiddo. The tension between Israel and Egypt is older than Moses; the Crusades were a manifestation of the tensions in the land bridge between continents. Long before oil added its fuel to the flames, the area was explosive.

Or consider Russia—the brooding presence that gives us no peace. Machiavelli might have had Khrushchev in mind when he wrote of a ruler who "never preaches anything but peace and good faith, and to both he is hostile, and either, if he kept it, would have deprived him of reputation and kingdom many a time."

John Quincy Adams, William H. Seward, and others sought to have a shield between the United States and Russia. And Alexis de Tocqueville, a century and a quarter ago, saw the inevitable tension. "To achieve its objective, America relies on personal interest and gives full rein to the strength and reason of the individual. Russia centers all authority of society in a single man. . . . Their points of departure are different, they follow different paths. None the less, each of them seems intended through some secret design of Providence to hold in its hands the destinies of half the world."

Henry Adams, no optimist, but sometimes a shrewd observer, remarked that Russians had "the single idea that Russia must fatally roll—must by her irresistible inertia crush whatever stood in her way." He also worried lest the "vast force of inertia known as China was to be united with the huge bulk of Russia in a single mass which no amount of new force could henceforth deflect."

Heinrich Heine quoted the words of Napoleon from St. Helena that "in the not too distant future the world will become an American republic or a Russian universal monarchy. . . . What a prospect!" Russia wanted warm water long before we became the symbol of her stalemate. The Bosporus she coveted, the Persian Gulf, the Japan Sea. In every direction there was an explosive expansionism, probing first in one direction, then another, long, long ago.

The problem of a divided Germany is older than Bismarck. Always there have been states fearful of the energy, the drive, the skill—and the power—of a united nation. Germany has been atomized before; it has been divided, shackled, and held in check. The astonishing thing to observe is that today two of the classic antagonists, France and Germany, are cooperating in many ways. One traditional rival—Britain—is allied with Germany. Only Russia bars the road to freedom and union now.

The Balkans have been a powder keg time out of mind. We should remind ourselves that the First World War started in what is now Jugoslavia. The tension between Greek and Turk is traditional.

Add Korea and Taiwan to the roll of the places where peace is endangered. In every instance the roots run deep in human history. Each offers problems in geopolitics, economics, racial hatreds, power balances, political instability, which date back many, many years.

Even Africa is not a new problem. It was the battleground of Moslem and Christian. It was so turbulent, so unruly that it stirred even the pacifist Thomas Jefferson to fight, though he had wanted to beach the Navy.

There is, I insist, no area of present peril where danger has not made its home, not once, but many times before. So I cannot find it in my heart to offer you sympathy, for in facing these problems you and your generation have instruments and assets more nearly equal to the task than your forebears, whose problems may have been less complex, less massive—but not in relation to their instruments and assets. Let us glance at some of those instrumentalities. I will pass over with barest mention new means of communication of all sorts—by word, by travel, by transportation—and also a thousand other technological advances.

Agriculture has undergone such a revolution that hunger need no longer stalk the earth. Where famine lingers, it is due to ignorance, to archaic land tenure, to political obscurantism.

Production processes have made such striking advances that "common labor" gives promise of becoming a rarity. Automation is a new word, but its substance began to appear years ago. Present refinements and acceleration are sensational, but logical, outcomes of long-known principles.

As late as the First World War we were a debtor nation, importing capital. Now we have wealth enough to be the banker of the world.

The most sensational growth in assets is almost never mentioned in talking of international relations. In the years of this century—not quite sixty—the expectation of life in America has increased twenty years—this despite the casualties of two world wars and the Korean strife. As against most nations in Asia and Africa, this means a normal expectation of thirty to forty years longer for you than for them. The advantage over life expectancy in parts of Europe, while not so great, is nonetheless significant.

This has a dominant relationship to the next asset—education. Relatively long life and great wealth combine to make possible spending many years in education, prolonging the period when you are not economically productive because your productiveness is not required, and because of the hope (expectation) that longer education will make you yet more productive and that longer life will compound that gain. Though these relationships have seldom been mentioned, much less stressed, they are very real and exceedingly important.

It is hard for you to realize that university education (in the modern sense) is only about eighty years old in this country. The generation which produced and the generation which fought the First World War had no instruction whatever in international relations and not much political science. The generation which produced and most of those who fought in the Second World War were somewhat—but not greatly—better off. Since that war the amount of advanced instruction in this area is almost beyond belief, especially in quantity, but also in quality.

Intellectuals tend to snarl at the radio, television, and other media of mass communication for their lack of emphasis upon education. Relative to what they might do, relative to what I would like to have them do, there is room for criticism and complaint. But speaking in realistic terms, we must acknowledge that what they actually do has made available, not only to some elite class, but to all the people, facts, opinions—enlightenment—which make democracy a more practicable form of government than ever before.

It is fashionable just now to lament the ignorance and the apathy of citizens. One of the most widely-read commentators, one with long and intimate experience in international affairs, both as participant and observer, lays what he conceives to be the decline of the West to the control of policy by public opinion. Politicians move "only as they placate, appease, bribe, seduce, bamboozle or otherwise manage to manipulate the demanding and threatening elements in their constituencies."[3] In a word, democracy and foreign policy do not mix.

If this is true, our goose is cooked. For better or worse, we are committed to democracy. Moreover, we can concede many of its inherent weaknesses without despair, for there is truth in what Churchill is quoted as saying—that it is the poorest kind of government except for every other sort. If you must be a pessimist, as a minimum agree that democracy is the "least worst." If you cannot agree to that, you will be following a dictum

---
[3] Walter Lippmann, *The Public Philosophy*, Boston, 1955.

of Hitler who insisted that "the great strength of a totalitarian state is that it forces those who fear it to imitate it." As you hear people advocate that we take our cue and our pace from the Soviets, think on those words of Hitler and ask yourself if you want to validate the dogma of a charlatan.

Perhaps I should not put the issue so bluntly. But why not? It is part of the record that authoritarian government appeals to two sorts: those who are eager to be the authorities, and those who are eager to escape thought. Democracy is founded on the optimistic faith that men will endure the agonies of thought in order to be free. And that is the issue each of you in your day and generation must face anew—just as every earlier generation has had to face it before you. And when democracy—or the progress toward it—has given way to totalitarianism —or the road to it—the failure has not been that of democracy but of citizenry.

Too many are like the popular sexton of a large parish. He got on with the parson, the deacons, the ladies' societies, the young people's groups—with everyone. At last a curious person asked him the secret. "It's simple; I put my mind in neutral and go where I am pushed." Passivity was no invention of his. You can read in Scripture of those who were "blown about by every wind of doctrine"—people with minds in neutral. That is one way to default upon your opportunities and responsibilities.

There is a second way in which you can defease your obligation as citizens and nullify your long and costly education. You can let your emotions dominate your opinions—and pretend to intelligence by rationalizing conclusions reached emotionally. The late Robert Sherwood belonged to a generation with no training for international affairs. I stood at the back of a crowded theater to watch his play, "Idiot's Delight," which had a long run on Broadway. It proved conclusively that war is never worth while. Then came the assault upon Finland by Russia and he wrote a second "standing room only" play, "There Shall Be No Night." It proved convincingly that war is sometimes essential. By the time the second play was on Broadway, the first had been Hollywooded and came to Broadway on film. So here was a playwright conducting a great debate with himself—two plays, equally powerful, each cancelling the conclusion of the other.

I admired and respected Robert Sherwood, and I stress the fact again that he, unlike you, belonged to an era whose sons were not educated in this field. You can plead no such excuse if you substitute feeling for thought.

There is a third escape from the obligation of rigorous thought—you can find scapegoats. Personalize everything. Explain the world in terms of angels or devils; tie a label on each world actor and hold him responsible.

Nehru is a muddle-headed, insincere politician; Nehru is a Moses leading a subcontinent out of colonialism through a wilderness.

Nasser is an Egyptian Hitler; Nasser is a rescuer of a nation from a rounder like Farouk.

Dulles is a great mind, a great moral force, a negotiator without peer; Dulles is a great bore, full of empty preachments, eager to do it all himself, clumsy in public relations.

Khrushchev is infinitely clever; Khrushchev is merely crafty, cynical—a new Stalin.

I am not denying that personalities are important and *occasionally* decisive. But political leadership is partly real and partly a mirage. Whether you agree with my optimistic outlook upon the relationship of democracy to foreign affairs, or the pessimistic bent of others, perhaps more entitled to speak than I, you must agree that men do not lead where no one follows; and politicians, even in totalitarian countries, sound out their followership before they indulge in leadership. In the simplest terms that means that all personalities work within limitations that are very real—very obvious in democracies, almost as real though less obvious in totalitarian nations. Personalizing events, therefore, is a misreading of the realities.

There is yet a fourth escape from thought about international matters. It is the most common escape route taken by educated men.

It is possible to equip yourself with a full complement of terms and phrases. These you can toss about with the subtle slyness characteristic of a name-dropper. By this method, you can conduct discussions, *apparently* intelligent, without the quiver of a neuron. These words and phrases are mostly colorful metaphors. When they were coined, they were useful in dramatizing and illuminating some complex reality, for which they came to stand as symbols. Then continuous, *unthinking* repetition made them appear not merely as symbols but as reality itself. When a metaphor undergoes that transformation, it becomes a distortion. Far from lighting up a dark spot, it blacks it out.

"Iron curtain" is such a phrase. It was a brilliant use of metaphor. But now it is repeated as though it were real, as though it were physically impossible to penetrate it. Yet daily thirty per cent of the students in the free university in the Western Sector of Berlin come from the Russian Zone—East Berlin. The elevated railways run on regular schedule right through this impenetrable shield. The two sectors have common water works, sewage disposal, telephone service. At the working level, the government of West Berlin and that of East Berlin have many essential contacts and reach understandings on practical matters. This has gone on for years.[4] The phrase, as originally used, dramatized a truth; thoughtlessly used, it conceals truth.

"Power vacuum" is another expression that can be tossed about without any necessity for thought. In the nineteenth and early twentieth centuries it was not only a useful expression; it put reality into strong terms. Now it is often a manifestation of unconscious imperialism; this happens when it carries the hidden assumption that a great nation must dominate every area—that small nations have no valid independence. Without power, there is no reality; such is the inference. As the head of one of the weaker states remarked plaintively: "A vacuum indicates that no one is here; we are!"

Those who view all parts of the world as adhering to Russia as to one magnetic pole or to us as a contrary pole display this thoughtless imperialism. They deny the reality of neutral independence. That is why the phrase "power vacuum," thoughtlessly employed, is vicious.

"Cold war," when first used, was brilliant in its implications. It reflected the hostility that underlay nearly every contact; it showed contrariety in the ideological, the economic, the armament assumptions and the intensity, the implacability of the enmity. It dramatized the need for a kind of peace which victory not only did not achieve, but did not even facilitate.

Time has corroded it; its thoughtless repetition led us

---
[4] Obviously this was written before the wall was erected in 1961.

to the folly of gagging scientists, finding disloyalty where it did not exist—as well as where it did. For long it made contacts between people have some of the moral opprobrium of "trading with the enemy." Its common use so distorts and misrepresents reality as to defeat all effort to comprehend our true position vis-à-vis the Soviets.

"Summit conference" was a characteristically Churchillian phrase, appropriate in the context in which he first used it. It has become a cyclone cellar for men who do not want to exert themselves in thought. What was once dramatic has become overdramatic. It now conceals the substance of the matter. If achievement is really at the summit, we follow totalitarian techniques. That is why Khrushchev maneuvers so continuously to attain it. If such a meeting is merely a device to project dramatically what is already virtually consummated through normal diplomatic channels, it smacks more of showmanship than of statesmanship.

This is why Lester Pearson, Nobel Prize winner, said, "What I plead for is no spectacular meeting of a Big Two, or a Big Three, or a Big Four at the summit, where the footing is precarious and the winds blow hard, but for a frank, serious and complete exchange of views—especially between Moscow and Washington—through diplomatic and political channels."

The next such phrase is the most disastrous of all when used as a substitute for thought—"the East-West struggle." It makes all the evil assumptions implicit in the "power vacuum" and adds others. If Russia and Red China are "East," where are India, Southeast Asia? Where is Africa? Omitting Africa is a large omission—200,000,000 people. Also omitted are Central and South America or, worse yet, they are taken for granted.

Now for a word—not a phrase—"disengagement."

Here is a harbor for all who would bandy terms without mental effort. Its proponent had an idea; he worked hard to think his way through it, and labored to expound it clearly.[5] In common use, however, it has become synonymous with retreat. "Retreat" is a plain, simple, crude word which no one can misunderstand. Therefore it has psychological disadvantages. "Disengagement" is a long, complicated, polysyllabic noun that helps obfuscate thought. Being a new word, it appears to meet the requirement trumpeted by politicians for "bold, imaginative, resourceful thinking." In reality, it is mere alteration in terminology; it is no longer thinking at all—just a verbal trick.

It is reminiscent of the advertisements, "This is an all new car." The automobile is new, indeed, since it is not made of secondhand parts; it has new and more tasteless, garish decor; but it is not new in engineering concepts, basic design, operating structure. The statement "This is an all new car" is literally true, but it is designed to leave a false inference in the mind as a residue. One of my friends told me that he employed public relations counsel. He did this, he said, to help him tell the truth in a misleading way. As a conversational gambit, "disengagement" now has all these qualities.

One last phrase requires discussion. If you want to talk learnedly without thought, it is your final refuge. Speak of the "national interest." So long as you do not define it, so long as you leave your hearer to fill the words with his own meaning, you can evade the pains of ratiocination.

One hearer will think you mean it in terms of total security, being armed to the teeth, possessing military superiority in all weapons systems and instant readiness

---
[5] George Kennan in the Reith Lectures, 1957-1958.

to fight at the click of a univac. Another, in the same group of hearers, will conceive of the national interest in economic terms. He realizes—or thinks he does—that national bankruptcy and national impotence are synonymous terms. He will say that a prosperous world will inevitably be non-Communist. In so saying, in his economic determinism he will be as Marxian as Marx himself.

Economic interpretation of the national interest to someone else in the group is the "sum of local interests." We must not have a Trade Agreements Act because the Japanese can make clothespins cheaper than Vermonters; cloth can be woven abroad cheaper than in Rhode Island; the Swiss can make better watches than Americans who have not half tried. We must have free enterprise—except when competition hurts; then the definition of free enterprise is government subsidy; but it must never be called that. Call it parity payment, call it tariff, call it quotas. Call it what you will so long as you do not call it subsidy.

This man can shut his eyes to reality here and dogmatize about conditions abroad. He will be one who scolds at Nehru for using the word "socialism," and denounces the overemphasis upon "the public sector" of the Indian economy. But he will close his eyes to the size of the public sector here—in farm supports, housing subsidies, expenditures for arms and research in those fields. He will never measure which nation has the largest public sector lest he be disconcerted. For as you do not want to be forced to define the national interest, he does not want to be forced to define free enterprise. You and he enter into a mutual conspiracy of silence about definitions, lest either be caught thinking—unawares.

Another man, when you use the phrase "national interest," will interpret it in psychological terms. He would move the State Department from Foggy Bottom to Madison Avenue, and outpropagandize the Soviets. He would have us develop a consistent "image," sloganize it, and drench an unwilling world with endless repetition. It would have the ingredients three out of four doctors recommend, and would taste good in a conspicuously ungrammatical way.

Yet another, in hearing you speak of the national interest, will give it a social connotation. Hindu, Moslem, Christian, Jew, Buddhist, Shintoist—all must forget their differences and stress their common elements and call them unity. He will remember that we accept varied pigmentation of everything but skin with no trouble. From toenails all the way up to hair, any color will do, blood red at the bottom, bright blond at the top—eyes can be gray, green, blue, brown, black. Why discriminate against skin?

At least one man who hears you speak of the national interest conceives of it in political terms. One of the most famous of the widely-read commentators wants to have a superelite diplomatic service of about 150 men—no more. Let them meet with elite diplomats from the other great powers and drop this nonsense of popular diplomacy.

I will not further multiply instances of escape from thought; instead let me summarize and conclude:

Yours is not the first generation to face daunting problems. Washington fought the Revolution—a bitter struggle, almost lost again and again. He saw the government of the Confederation totter—bankrupt and impotent. He gave silent but powerful leadership to the Constitution and organized the new government, setting precedents with exceeding care. He came to retirement and had prepared a Farewell Address. In it he said, "*If* we remain one people"; we read those words as though they meant nothing, but they expressed a real doubt, a haunting fear. That was fourteen years after independence was won. Yet today we want to toss in the sponge over Pakistan, Burma, Indonesia, none of which is that old.

Lincoln endured the agonies of the War Between the States. His election precipitated it; he bore a great responsibility. At Gettysburg, he said the nation was conceived in liberty and dedicated to the proposition that all men are created equal. The war, he said, was a test whether any nation so conceived and so dedicated could long endure, and whether government of the people, by the people, for the people would perish from the earth. Those were not the calculated and polished phrases of a politician, or ghost-written eloquence, but the heartfelt outburst of a man who had seen the nation on the brink of destruction—eighty years after the end of the Revolution.

This, then, is not the first time democracy has been in trouble. It is the first time much of the world has had the opportunity to try it. If it falters, is it any wonder?

Second, your generation is not the first to find pessimism dominant. It is a reaction from the inflated hopes of the First World War—called a war to end war, a war to make the world safe for democracy. As surely as gloom has settled, the tide will turn and optimism will have its day again.

Third, you are the first to be given the opportunity to know, to be trained, to have available time, wealth, and instruments equal to the problems.

The only need is courage—the courage to think, the

courage to be patient, to outwait our opponents when the course we have set is right. That program has paid off before now. The nervous Nellies said the Soviets would "never" let go of Austria; the wise commentators pleaded that we should take some fresh initiative. For eight years there appeared to be a permanent sterile stalemate—then a sudden opportunity opened and Austria was free and independent.

The Saar basin was an old bone of contention between France and Germany. Its situation, its value, its symbolic importance made yielding by either side "impossible." But its status was settled amicably.

As Ambassador Conant remarked after retiring from his post in Germany, such progress seems "to prove the old saying that it is darkest before the dawn; what I think it actually proves is the difficulty of predicting when the dawn will break . . . and wise statesmen are those who intuitively make the calculation and are ready to take advantage of the impending change from night to day. *For when that occurs, what has been literally impossible proves to be miraculously easy.* Generalizations based on a long experience in an arctic night have no applicability for the summer months when visibility is high."[6]

I will not deny that the night is dark, or that it has been long. But unless human experience has been meaningless, dawn will break—not all at once everywhere, but in one place after another. If your nerves are steady, your mind clear, and your will firm, you will be ready to seize that opportunity and exploit it to the full.

---
[6] James Bryant Conant, *Germany and Freedom,* Cambridge, 1958. Italics supplied.

VII ⁐ The Age of Revolution

OF THE many roads by which a private citizen may approach consideration of international relations, three are worthy of particular mention: knowledge, emotion, imagination. The last of these—imagination—deserves special thought, for it offers extremely useful help in dealing with a turbulent world, and above all with the acutely disturbed new and underdeveloped nations.

Knowledge is the first method of approach; the process for its creation is scholarship. This is the way to develop the specialist, a person who knows a great deal about some aspect of policy in time or space or thought—or all three. Such work is essential to progress in the quest for peace. Without specialists statesmen would lack access to essential knowledge. Not all citizens can be scholars; they have other preoccupations. But all citizens can profit by the research of scholars, for the work of many is summarized and synthesized by secondary writers. Essential knowledge is made available in palatable form, and every citizen should learn as much as possible. Above all, he should think about what he

FOREIGN AFFAIRS, July 1961. (Copyright 1961 by the Council on Foreign Relations, Inc., New York. Reprinted by permission.)

knows. One historical fact, in particular, should enter his consciousness and become firmly fixed: there never was a golden age when men lived happily, securely, without tensions.

When we read history, events are foreshortened. A century or more of progress may be covered in a sentence or two. Thus it seems as though the meaning of events must have been obvious to those who lived among them. But that is a rare occurrence; the normal rule is that only in the long perspective does the significance of the age become clear. A verse in Ecclesiastes reminds us how old is this problem: "For man also knoweth not his time: as the fishes that are taken in an evil net, and as the birds that are caught in the snare; so are the sons of men snared in an evil time." One of the fundamentals a citizen must grasp is that every age has had its problems, its dangers, even its moments of desperation.

The second approach to foreign affairs is emotional. This road is hard packed, for it has been well traveled by idealists. No one with any sensitiveness can look out upon the world without acute awareness of the prevalence of hunger amounting to starvation, poverty almost beyond belief, disease, misery, degradation of life itself. These things prevail among the vast majority.

Those whose responses are primarily emotional will be tempted to make a direct, naïve assault upon these evils. Such sentimentalism is self-defeating; it retards reform by offending those whom it is intended to help. Nonetheless, all impulse to action has its roots in the emotions. As the citizen who tries to be effective in shaping public opinion must seek knowledge, so also he must draw inspiration to action from emotion.

Imagination is the third method by which a citizen

can be effective in forming sound public opinion regarding foreign relations. Imagination is not dreaming; by definition dreams are unreal. Imagination can be, and must be, disciplined. Those who wish to strengthen their imaginative powers will draw not only on knowledge, but also on idealism, the urge "to do something about it." They will go further; imaginative citizens will remember that a stranger's pattern of thought and action, even his value judgments, are largely inherited. They may be modified by skill and patience, but the process cannot be hurried.

Patience must, therefore, be a principal ingredient in the discipline of the imagination. Only by the cultivation of almost infinite patience can the citizen escape the defeatism that arises when the initial effort fails to produce perfection. Such lack of patience tends to be characteristic of journalists; it explains their prevailing pessimism. They look for "news," particularly "hard" news, something dramatic, decisive. They do not usually observe the slow process of evolutionary change because their perspective is too short. Even if they could catch the drift, they would not think it worth a line of type because it lacks "impact." Thus much of the solid progress of the world goes unreported.

The man of disciplined imagination will be happy with progress which, though small, astonishes the scholar, while its slow pace will dismay the sentimentalist. Ignorance, disease, poverty, hunger are not the fruits of imperialism, or colonialism, or the industrial revolution. They are as old as mankind and will not be banished easily or swiftly. That is not pessimism; it is a summons to patience.

In the discipline of imagination, persistence comes

next to patience. As patience realizes that great results will not be easy, persistence appreciates that even slow progress will grind to a halt unless effort is vigorous and continuous.

If the idea be accepted that a vivid and disciplined imagination is a valid instrument by which the private citizen can think constructively about foreign affairs, we can offer six illustrations of how it can be applied to our relationships with the newly independent, the anciently ignorant, the shockingly poor, and the sadly diseased nations of world.

The first necessity is to rid ourselves of nervousness when "revolution" is mentioned. Politicians often shy like skittish horses at the mere word. This is nonsensical. Thomas Jefferson once wrote in a letter: "What country before ever existed a century and a half without a revolution? . . . the tree of liberty must be refreshed from time to time with the blood of patriots and tyrants. It is its natural manure."

The slightest acquaintance with history makes it clear that revolutions are as old as recorded history—and as current as today's news. The Cromwellian era in Britain was revolutionary; that should remind us that even the most stable institutions have from time to time been shaken to their foundations. The United States broke its ties with the mother country by revolution, and far from being ashamed of the fact, our forefathers made it a matter of pride. Our War Between the States was long and costly in life as well as treasure.

Since the eighteenth century, revolution has been endemic in France. In the latest successful instance, when de Gaulle swept into power, legal forms were meticulously followed and violence was latent rather than overt, but the substance of the change was revolution. A series of revolutions occurred in Italy and in Germany in both the nineteenth and twentieth centuries, and the same has been true in Russia. If the well-developed, relatively stable parts of the world have experienced so many explosive changes, there is no reason to be astonished that revolution is not merely endemic but epidemic in Asia, Africa, and Latin America.

It is easy to assert that all changes in government should be achieved by ballots instead of bullets, but the realities of human experience make that a mere wish-fancy which a well-disciplined imagination must reject. So common has been revolutionary change that there is a considerable body of literature in its defense. The United States is the source of some of the most eloquent pleas for the legitimacy of revolution. Even a state we regard as conservative, New Hampshire, put this passage in its Constitution of 1792: "The doctrine of non-resistance against arbitrary power and oppression is absurd, slavish, and destructive of the good and happiness of mankind." Read again the Declaration of Independence where, among the "causes" of our Revolution, appears this statement: "That whenever any Form of Government becomes destructive of these ends, it is the Right of the People to alter or to abolish it, and to institute new Government, laying its foundation on such principles and organizing its powers in such form, as to them shall seem most likely to effect their Safety and Happiness."

It would be difficult to find more persuasive defenses of revolution. Such statements, too often forgotten or neglected in the United States, are quoted frequently in the new nations. Read aright, our Declaration of Independence makes us kin to all the new nations that have escaped from the status of wards and attained the stature of independence.

Our own interest in revolution did not wane when we achieved independence, nor did we regard it as a blessing appropriate to ourselves alone. From the days of Washington almost to the presidency of Wilson our recognition policy reflected that interest. Jefferson put it in these words: "We surely cannot deny to any nation that right wherein our own government is founded—that one may govern itself according to whatever form it pleases and change these forms at its own will.... The will of the nation is the only thing essential to be regarded."

We rejoiced in Kossuth's effort to make Hungary free in 1849. At that time Daniel Webster said the United States could not be indifferent to "the fortunes of nations struggling for institutions like our own. Certainly the United States may be pardoned ... if they entertain an ardent affection for those popular forms of political organization which have so rapidly advanced their own prosperity and happiness." In our current mood his words seem bombastic, but at the time they evoked passionate approval, for they expressed a profound urge to see the whole world free. Lincoln spoke for every American when he described the Declaration of Independence as "a stumbling block to tyrants," giving "hope to all the world, for all future time. It was that which gave promise that in due time the weight would be lifted from the shoulders of all men." It would be easy to compile a long list of instances when, with public support, the government of the United States welcomed and encouraged revolution.

Familiarity with our own record will end much of the difficulty in understanding current revolutions. For 1961 is still part of the Age of Revolution that was launched in 1776. Once the citizen has become accustomed to this idea, there will be no temptation to bewail all violent political change. The first essential in an imaginative approach to new governments, therefore, is to realize that revolution is normal, sanctified by experience and by theory.

The second step in the imaginative understanding of new governments is a realization that they will be unstable, that there will be keen competition to govern. The reasons lie plain upon the surface. During a struggle for independence all patriots can unite upon that one common goal, subordinating their differences to the single paramount objective. Deficiencies that have existed in the public service, of whatever sort, can be attributed to the imperial power, taxes can be blamed upon the distant rulers, and every burden can be described as "exploitation." Our Declaration of Independence contained a whole catalogue of abuses.

Once independence is achieved, all that is changed. Unity of purpose can no longer be attained by fighting against an outsider; no distant devil can be blamed. There must now be purpose for, not against, and every man is likely to have his own program.

Again our own history illustrates the problem perfectly. Thomas Paine, one of the authors of our Revolution, whose "Appeal to Reason" was such a potent force, was as one with Washington throughout the war. But in 1796, Paine wrote in a pamphlet entitled "Letter to George Washington": "There was a time when the fame of America, moral and political, stood fair and high in the world. The luster of her revolution extended itself to every individual and to be a citizen of America gave a title to respect in Europe. Neither meanness nor ingratitude had then mingled itself into the composition of her character. . . . The Washington of politics had not then appeared. . . . And as to you, sir, treacherous in private friendship . . . and a hypocrite in public life, the world will be puzzled to decide, whether you are an apostate or an impostor; whether you have abandoned good principles, or whether you ever had any."

The rift after our Revolution was not merely personal; it was revealed in the structure of government. The colonies, having become states, set up a central government, but they had been resisting centralized control and saw to it that it was weak. The Articles of Confederation were slow in the drafting (seventeen months), tardy in acceptance (over three years), feeble in action. Our first national government was a failure.

From the Declaration of Independence to the establishment of our second government in 1789, nearly thirteen years elapsed. Even then we had not fully faced reality. The new Constitution made no reference to political parties, which Washington and others denounced, calling them factions. Yet between the ideas of Jefferson on the one hand and Hamilton on the other there was a great gulf which neither all the efforts nor all the persuasion nor all the prestige of Washington could bridge. Parties proved to be essential to the operation of the government.

If, with all the inheritance from British constitutional tradition and all the training in self-government which our forefathers possessed, they could not remain united, how can we expect the new nations, most of which have no such sound background, to do better? At the end of thirteen years of declared independence, our government was virtually bankrupt. Even after the federal government was set up and fiscal order restored, as late as 1800, Aaron Burr was almost able to steal the presidency from Jefferson. Few Americans now recall that Jefferson finally won only on the thirty-sixth ballot. It took a constitutional amendment to prevent a recurrence of so scandalous a gambit—and to admit thereby how essential a role political parties play.

Yet we tend to feel upset if new nations and new governments, none of which are yet so old as we were in 1789, show evidences of instability, rivalry among leaders, fiscal disorder—in short the same symptoms we exhibited in our own infant days. In summary, the second point which the imaginative approach must stress in thinking about new nations is that instability is inherent in post-revolutionary states.

A third characteristic of new governments, which imagination should help us understand, is the relationship of the new rulers to their political opponents. During our political campaigns, candidates denounce each other on the hustings; election over, they meet amiably. The transition from one administration to another is extraordinarily smooth. We take it for granted that foreign ambassadors will maintain social relations with leaders of opposition parties, and if, before our election, the British ambassador had not been acquainted with Adlai Stevenson, Lyndon Johnson, and Sam Rayburn, we would have felt he was not up to his job. Similarly, our ambassador in the United Kingdom, as a matter of course, knows Hugh Gaitskell and Harold Wilson.

In revolutionary situations, different rules apply, for the opposition is not a "loyal opposition" or merely a political competitor; it is the enemy. The defeated opponent is likely to be plotting the overthrow of the government and may be assembling clandestine armed forces. In these circumstances, a revolutionary leader will not look with calm upon social or personal relations between foreign ambassadors and his opponents. The effort to maintain such contacts may well lead to the diplomat being declared *persona non grata*.

Again our own history should assist in understanding this problem. When the new governments curb such normal social contacts on grounds of "internal security," we should recall the dismissal of Citizen Genêt by Washington. We should remember, also, the Alien and Sedition Acts during the administration of John Adams. Like much legislation in today's new states, those acts were aimed at suppressing political opposition. We hope we have outgrown such maneuvers, but the feelings which motivated them survive in the United States today.

It required all our political sophistication to treat Khrushchev, when he came here the first time, not as the author of savagery in Hungary, but as the leader of a great power with which the realities of international life required us to deal. His second trip produced many hostile manifestations. If it is so hard for us to exhibit restraint, we ought to be able to understand the oversensitiveness of weak, new governments menaced by an opposition ready to resort to bullets at the first hope of success.

An imaginative approach should help us grasp a fourth fundamental point about revolutions. Revolution, as the word itself suggests, is like turning a wheel. Start a wheel and momentum takes over to some extent; it rarely stops—except in closely controlled circumstances—just where you want it to.

Even revolutionary leaders who are pure in heart, dedicated in purpose, democratic in ideals, cannot make the wheel spin and stop exactly 180 degrees from the starting point. Their energies may prove deficient and move the wheel not at all—or only 90 degrees. The wheel may turn full circle—360 degrees—which, in another context, is one revolution. The French Revolution spun all the way from the Bourbons clear around to Napoleon. Revolutions develop a dynamic of their own, and no one can predict just how far they will go. The righteousness of the initial impulse does not always govern the result.

Victory is heady wine. One who has ever lived on a college campus understands this, for he has observed the behavior of students at the moment of a football victory—exuberant, irrational, abandoned. It is the more intense when the team's record has not been good, and when some break in the game or a dramatic surge has brought victory when defeat seemed imminent. The emotional release is violent. If, with the long tradition of sportsmanship which exercises rigid control over normal behavior, so much ungoverned emotional energy is loosed over what is, relative to the great events of the world, so minor an occasion, how much more readily can we understand the intoxication that follows success in bringing an end to tyranny at imminent risk of life. No wonder it often produces wild excesses.

The fifth aspect of revolution we can also apprehend imaginatively: victors do not take kindly to advice. In gaining independence, they were "do-it-yourself" men. Many leaders in the world today, and virtually all the revolutionaries, have been in prison, in exile, or in great personal danger: Bourguiba, Nkrumah, de Gaulle, Adenauer, Gomulka, Tito, Nasser, Diem, Nehru, Sukarno, Castro—and many more. Most of them owe no thanks to armchair critics that they are now in power rather than in graves.

The colonial revolutionaries, especially, feel no gratitude to outsiders. Indeed, did we not do business with their late masters and so "help the enemy"? We gave money and military goods to many of the former rulers, and though our motives were pure and we did not intend to help hold colonies in subjection or suppress revolution, the net result of our aid often was to strengthen the metropolitan power or the predecessor government. And despite our historic anti-colonialism, we have not been wholly free, since we became a world-wide power, to exhibit our real feelings. Our relations with Europe—the necessity for maintaining alliances—sometimes conflicted with our desire for the liquidation of colonialism in Asia and Africa. We urged the Netherlands so strongly to give independence to Indonesia that we strained our relations with that key nation in Europe, yet our diplomatic pressure was neither so overt nor so dramatic as aid to the Netherlands through the Marshall Plan and NATO. Sukarno was aware of our tangible help to his enemy; our intangible diplomatic pressure was not so visible.

Moreover, revolutionary leaders are under severe domestic pressures. In rallying their own people to make sacrifices for the revolution, they made promises, explicit or implicit. They cannot now exercise power without making major changes. It may well be that the first need of the new country is wiser use of the land, improved breeds of hens to lay more eggs, better cows to give more milk. But that does not mean that such programs will have priority, for they are not dramatic and their results appear too gradually to satisfy people whose expectations have been inflated. Having achieved something great and dynamic in the moment of revolution, the new leader cannot ask his people to wait for evolutionary processes to mature over a long period of time. He is the symbol of action, not of more eggs! He will resent counsel to move slowly. As a man of wide experience has put it, we must expect that "new governments may sometimes insist on types of growth which have more to do with prestige than need." The "revolution of rising expectations" has often, therefore, more of the dramatic than the necessary.

Independence, we must remember, means freedom to do the wrong thing as well as the right. That ought not to be a difficult concept to grasp, for we have pursued farm policies, for example, which pile up bigger and bigger food surpluses and higher and higher costs and deficits. Those policies add up to economic folly, but have been thought to be politically profitable. Clearly, we are in no position to be overly censorious of those who, with less experience, less training, and fewer resources, make mistakes which seem to us serious.

The argument that the development of new nations should be left to private capital—or to "free enterprise"—will fall on deaf ears. The word "socialism," far from holding terrors for them, has deep attraction. The leaders of new states know that most of the free nations of the world have now, or have had, socialist governments. Many of them are more aware than we appear to be that our own economy is a mixture—that government plays a large role in our economic life. The Tennessee Valley Authority is one of our most conspicuous exports. Our railroads were built with heavy government subsidy, and many want more now. Our canals and waterways are all public enterprises, and in most free nations so are railroads and telephones—and the universities.

These men who engineered revolution want now to manage the economy. They remember that the hated imperial control followed in the train of private trade and investment. We tend to think that the normal sequence is for trade to follow the flag, but their own history tells them that it was often the other way round. The Belgian Congo started as a private speculation of King Leopold, who became fabulously wealthy without notable benefit to the Africans. The Indonesians saw the Dutch grow rich, while they remained poor. This experience, many times repeated in many places around the world, created the image—still dominant today—of capitalism as exploitation. New governments view with deep suspicion, therefore, great capitalistic enterprises coming from abroad. Having once found that process a prelude to colonialism, they are doubly shy.

Many of the new nations fear the rule of prices by a free market, for they are producers of raw materials—tin, rubber, coffee, tea, cocoa, jute, and so on. Asians can point to a United Nations calculation that in recent experience their reduced incomes from such exports, occasioned by falling prices in free markets, just about offset the grants-in-aid. They are also aware that the United States puts quotas on oil, zinc, copper, sugar, and that it deliberately sets out to defeat the free market in agriculture by government intervention. Why, they ask, should we be critical when they follow the same pattern of political suppression of economic forces?

Moreover, many new states have not the wealth to support free enterprise. There is no accumulation of domestic capital with which to finance industrial development. Poverty is so intense that domestic savings can be found only, as in Russia in Stalin's day or now in Red China, by grinding the faces of the poor and letting millions starve. If, therefore, the nation is not to become totalitarian, the money must come from abroad. But so sensitive are the new leaders that they will regard any advice, any cautionary devices connected with aid, as "strings."

The ordinary requirements which we all accept when borrowing money, they resent. They see them as manifestations of economic—and ultimately political—imperialism, and having just escaped from one form of dependence they do not want to fall into another. Our history ought to remind us that this is the normal mood of debtors. The resentments of our Western states at what was regarded as "Wall Street control" are classic. When mortgages were being foreclosed, the great Senator from Missouri, Thomas Hart Benton, exploded: "A lump of butter in the mouth of a dog, one gulp, one swallow, and all is gone." Many a Westerner in the mid-nineteenth century regarded that as the restrained statement of a moderate.

These things partially explain why our foreign aid program is not uniformly a success. We need to do many things better, but the point is missed completely by those who feel that if only we had a different organizational structure or more money or made this, that, or the other change in procedure, our troubles would disappear. There is no simple, easy way to achieve the desirable ends. We must do the best we can, profiting by experience, not endlessly repeating the same errors, but accepting, nevertheless, the inevitability of failure to attain Utopia in a short time. The growth of economic freedom, as of political freedom, is a slow process, with many painful setbacks.

Appreciation of the fact that each individual nation has a unique perspective upon history is a sixth way in which imagination can help the citizen grasp the realities of a revolutionary world. Depending upon the national points of view from which it is observed, the same historical event carries wholly different significances; what seems trivial to one appears vital to the other. Each nation tends to regard its version as "truth," overlooking the validity of other viewpoints.

When this national emphasis is forgotten, present difficulties are too often attributed to current or recent episodes, whereas the roots of trouble frequently lie deeper in divergent national interpretations of history. Such difficulties will not disappear rapidly, or be eliminated by some change in the style of our diplomacy. In South America, in Africa, and in Asia many nations feel that we are obsessed with the menace of Communism. We can justify that concern to ourselves, for we have experienced the retreat from Wilson's vision of a world safe for democracy, and have seen the rise of Soviet confidence that Marxism-Leninism will embrace the entire world.

The historical tradition of many nations makes other menaces—such as imperialism, economic or political—seem much more real. Their experience has not sensitized them to the Communist danger. When we try to transfer our justified alarm to them, they not only do not accept the warnings, they resent them. Our interest in their development is seen as an effort to draw them into a power struggle which they regard as irrelevant to their concerns.

One of the most striking instances of different national perspectives upon history—as a cause of profound misunderstanding—is the Monroe Doctrine. It has customarily been treated in our histories as a wholly defensive concept. From the standpoint of the United States, it was an anti-imperialist pronouncement designed to let the nations of this hemisphere develop without external interference. The angle of vision of Latin countries is different. When we undertook to speak on behalf of this hemisphere, it is undeniable that we "took Latin America for granted," since no nation had given us authorization to speak on its behalf. From the Latin point of view, we were at least impinging upon the policy formation of independent nations; to that extent we committed a trespass upon their sovereignty. It was a manifestation of the unconscious arrogance that arises from the consciousness of power. Inconceivable as it may seem to us that Monroeism could be identified with imperialism, for some Latin nations that identification seems natural.

Once this divergence in perspective is grasped imaginatively, many episodes which appear as almost insignificant in our history are seen to loom decisively large in theirs. To us Cuba is a small nation in which we have taken an avuncular interest. Cubans read history differently; for a century our statesmen spoke of the acquisition of the island as inevitable. Even after we decided against annexation, we retained control through the Platt Amendment, which limited the power of Cuba to act as a sovereign state and authorized intervention by the United States. We exercised that right from time to time, treating the Cubans as wards and determining who should govern them. The liquidation of the Platt Amendment did not occur until 1934. Cuban history stresses the reality of our control rather than the philanthropic purpose which our histories emphasize.

Mexicans recall our war with them in 1846-1848, as a consequence of which we took California, New Mexico, and parts of three states. President Polk asked for authority to occupy Yucatan; President Pierce arranged the Gadsden Purchase; President Buchanan proposed intervention and the occupation of two Mexican states. Even after the War Between the States there were considerable periods when Mexico lived in perpetual fear of invasion. Wilson twice invaded Mexico, and sought to determine who should be its president.

The United States acquired as many of the Caribbean islands as possible and wanted more. The purchase of the Virgin Islands was negotiated by Seward, and consummated in this century. We took over Puerto Rico from Spain. President Grant's acquisition of the Dominican Republic was defeated by the Senate, but later the finances of that republic were supervised by the United States, and it was militarily occupied and governed by us for some years. In 1915, during occupation by our Marines, a virtual American protectorate was established over Haiti by treaty; it went further than the Platt Amendment in establishing American control. Fiscal independence for the two republics was conceded only twenty years ago.

In 1880 President Hayes called the proposed Isthmian canal "virtually part of our coastline." To us that seemed logical enough; to others it looked like imperialism. The British commented that the President's view would deny the states in the vicinity of the canal "as independent a position as that which they now occupy." A Republican Secretary of State, James G. Blaine, spoke of a "long-established claim of priority on the American continent," and a Democratic Secretary of State, Richard Olney, announced that the United States was "practically sovereign on this continent and its fiat is law upon the subjects to which it confines its interposition." Later Secretary Philander C. Knox spoke of the area as "a portion of the world where the influence of the United States must naturally be preëminent." The word "naturally" was galling in the extreme, as were the earlier statements based upon our overwhelming power.

When Theodore Roosevelt said, "I took Panama," it seemed to us merely a brash statement about a regrettable episode. For Colombia and Panama it was an event decisive in their history, one which has bedevilled our relationships ever since.

The Roosevelt corollary to the Monroe Doctrine assigned the United States an international police power; we were to determine unilaterally when, where, and how much we should intervene. From the Latin point of view, we were saying, "Might makes right." The gospel of the corollary was followed by three administrations, the most extreme of which was that of President Wilson. He set out to "instruct" the Latin American republics in democracy. He held it "our peculiar duty" to teach them "to elect good men" and establish "order and self-control." He was willing to act in some cases "even if the sovereignty of unwilling nations be outraged in the process." Under the impulse of these dogmas, he violated the sovereignty of several nations, occupying some and controlling others.

The principal historian of the Monroe Doctrine has recorded that by 1915 Monroeism had "been deeply charged with an assumption of the right to control, of superior power, of hegemony over the other states of the New World."[1] How better describe imperialism?

To use a current term, we made satellites of a number of nations. From our standpoint, American imperialism was distinctive: we did not intend our control to be permanent but a transient phase during which the people for whom we accepted responsibility gained experience in self-government. In the second place, the element of exploitation inherent in classic imperialism, though not wholly absent, was subordinated to philanthropic purpose. The recipients of our unwelcome attentions, however, resented our assumption of superior virtue and did not accept at face value our protestations of good intentions. The management of satellites proved unrewarding; it did not produce desired results and it deeply implanted fear of "Yankee imperialism" throughout Latin America.

There is, indeed, a whole literature in Latin America

---
[1] Dexter Perkins, *Hands Off: A History of the Monroe Doctrine*, Boston, 1941.

which interpreted Monroeism as imperialism. As a consequence, when President Cleveland intervened in the Venezuelan boundary dispute, his initiative, instead of evoking support, was viewed with grave suspicion in Mexico, Chile, and Argentina. An Argentinian statesman, later president of that republic, championed Spain against the United States in 1898. When we presented resolutions in Pan American conferences, they often met with suspicion that we were seeking hegemony rather than defense of common interests. During the First World War the Mexican government was sympathetic to Germany.

We see the episodes mentioned and many others as marginal incidents in our history, and, in any event, part of a closed book. From our point of view, we have exchanged the expansive and imperialist dreams of earlier times for the status of counselor and friend, though our relationship to events in Guatemala in 1954 seemed to Latins to go much further. The one who exercises power and the one upon whom it is exercised almost always have a different interpretation of the motives involved. The slightest hint of condescension, even in connection with economic aid, is sure to evoke deep resentment. If we approach the matter imaginatively, we will not be surprised at the lingering fears of the Colossus of the North, or at the persistent suspicion that we have not wholly abandoned imperialist ambitions.

We think we have learned at great cost that we must not let dislike of political and social retrogression induce us actively to manage other people's affairs. We may use such diplomatic instruments as are available, but beyond that it is unwise to go except in concert with other nations through the Organization of American States or the

United Nations. Otherwise, we set ourselves up as moral imperialists, seeking to choose not only our own course of action but also to direct the lives of other nations.

Latin America illustrates the need imaginatively to remain constantly alert to the different historical perspectives of other people as we attempt to understand their prejudices and fears. What we sometimes take for jealousy of our might and our wealth is, to some extent, a reaction to unconscious arrogance when we speak all too glibly of "our position of leadership." Leadership should be a combination of wisdom, courage, and persuasiveness. The more fully we appreciate the folly of mistaking dominance for leadership, the sooner will the underdeveloped nations accept the sincerity of our purpose.

There has been a growing feeling that the problems of foreign affairs have become so complicated that the private citizen cannot be expected to understand them, much less make a positive contribution to their resolution. Concurrently there has been a surfeit of demands that Washington officials should develop "bold, new, imaginative policies and plans." This is tantamount to asking that those eminently desirable ends should be achieved in a vacuum. That is not only undesirable, it is impossible. We do not have a government of experts, and if we were to try to form one it would be utterly disastrous to the whole concept of democracy to which we are deeply committed. The expert has an essential but nonetheless a subordinate role to play; he can advise, but he cannot take the place of political leadership. By its very nature political leadership loses its effectiveness unless there is a significant degree of public consensus behind proposals for action. Many a novel and constructive idea, possibly conceived by experts but responsibility for which was accepted by a political leader, has come to nought for lack of intelligent popular support.

So long as the United States remains committed to the democratic process, there can be no substitute for effective citizenship. The development of that effectiveness with regard to foreign affairs depends to a great extent upon the application of imagination to help in achieving an understanding of events in the world. Long ago Aristotle argued that citizens need not be experts in order to exercise a sound judgment in public affairs. Time has proved him right. In practice, freshness of official thought is often stimulated by imaginative suggestions from individuals or groups of citizens. They are then ready to rally support for courageous alterations in old policies that time has made sterile.

VIII ∾ Thoughts for Tomorrow

In FOREIGN affairs today, both policy and performance require more subtlety and sophistication than heretofore. The need arises from no significant change in human relations, for the basic factors in man's relationship to himself and to other men have not altered radically. When we speak of "a new world" or "a new age," or employ one of the other current expressions, it brings more confusion than clarity to thought. During my own lifetime I have known the steel age, the air age, the age of science, the age of technology, the atomic age, the space age, or, on different levels, the age of democracy, the age of totalitarianism, the age of capitalism, the age of Communism, the age of peace, and the age of war. When ages shoot by at so rapid a clip the concept is worthless, and confusing.

It is indubitable that many physical changes in the world deeply affect our foreign relations. On the other hand, there are equally vital elements of continuity—things which change not at all or very slowly. Science and technology have altered much of our environment, but they have not remade the human mind or spirit.

FOREIGN AFFAIRS, April 1962. (Copyright 1962 by the Council on Foreign Relations, Inc., New York. Reprinted by permission.)

The charter of UNESCO declares that wars begin in the minds of men. The statement is suggestive, but inaccurate. Many of the things for which men have fought lie deep beneath thought processes; they are not rational at all. A more perceptive statement would have been that wars begin in the hearts of men, using "hearts" in the old-fashioned sense, meaning the passions, the will, the drives, the subconscious, the unconscious—all those forces of which psychoanalysis has made so much and for which it has devised so many terms. The word "heart" is so employed in the Scriptures over five hundred times; again and again it is referred to as the secret hiding place of the decisive impulses that move men. The specific things that men have feared and hated most ardently have changed from time to time and place to place, but of the continuing reality and power of the basic drives, now as before, there can be no question.

The first step—and it is a long one—toward a more sophisticated approach to the world we live in and will live in tomorrow is to recognize these hidden intangibles as continuing and often decisive factors in international relations. We have no Geiger counters with which to measure their intensity; no one has yet discovered a reliable test of the human will; we have no gauge to reveal at what point courage will falter. Each, from his own experience, knows that these traits are not fixed in either quantity or quality but vary with a multitude of moods and circumstances. Anyone who candidly examines why a single individual chooses to do one thing instead of another finds himself in a vast complex of interests and motives. Only with difficulty—and with a wide margin of error—do psychoanalysts discover them in individuals even when aided by willing cooperation.

With nations, the difficulty of finding simple explanations is raised to the nth power, since no couch is large enough for a whole people, no questions are adequately perceptive, and willing cooperation is conspicuously absent. Simple explanations of the behavior of nations should be treated not merely with skepticism but with outright disbelief. Naïve assumptions regarding such matters can throw policy fatally out of proper direction.

Forecasting the future has been one of man's favorite preoccupations. Almost from the beginning of recorded history seers and prophets, kings and potentates have proclaimed new eras in the history of mankind. In our own nation, even as seasoned a statesman as John Quincy Adams took for granted our ultimate ownership of Cuba. Many prominent statesmen used "manifest destiny" to predict the absorption of Canada and Mexico. The proclamations of Woodrow Wilson—a war to end war, a world safe for democracy—were stirring as war slogans but proved wide of the mark as prophecy. So were those of Franklin Roosevelt—"Our industrial plant is built." These forecasts followed an age-old tradition of similar errors.

Although each era is unlike those which preceded and those which followed, contemporaries almost never identified the dominant elements of their own time accurately. Things which seemed decisive to them proved in the long run to be transient or of relatively little significance. Changes which passed all but unnoticed by the men on the scene came, in the perspective of history, to be regarded as vital. If great leaders have proved unable to "discern the signs of the times," surely predictions based on alleged contemporary trends are unreliable.

In any event, dependence upon the persistence of trends in human affairs is based on a fallacy. It rests upon a false analogy with extrapolations that may be useful in statistics and engineering; and even those projections, though useful, are often fairly crude instruments. A scatter chart of data reveals clusters which appear to form a sort of pattern. A curve is drawn along the mean among the clustered data, neglecting those which deviate too far from the observed pattern. (I forbear to press the embarrassing and unanswerable question: how far is too far?) When the curve is drawn as far as the data in hand permit, it is projected forward upon the assumption that the pattern of the past supplies a probable pattern for the future.

When applied to questions of national policy, the extrapolation process breaks down at three points. First, the scatter chart cannot be composed of the closely defined sort of data used by statisticians and engineers. The data are disparate, not to say heterogeneous; therefore they would be more scattered than an engineer's chart. The curve along the mean would be much less trustworthy as an indication of a past trend, and its reliability as prediction even more speculative. Further, it is impossible, even with modern computers, to put down all relevant facts, for they are in number as the sands of the seas. Some must be selected and others neglected. No two equally competent people would make the same selection of what to include and what to omit. Two scatter charts based on different sets of data would show quite different patterns.

Forecasting on the basis of trends involves using history as a reference. Now history has much to teach us, but if we are usefully to exploit what it tells, we must recognize its limitations. The startling fact is that there are vast stretches of history which have never been written. Much past experience of great relevance is unavailable because we cannot possess answers to questions that have never been asked. Each generation tends to write about what interests it, which may have been of great importance in our past but may not be for our future. Much accumulated history is irrelevant to current and emergent problems.

Furthermore, history has a built-in bias. It deals with what was done and what was said by those who did it. It gives short shrift to alternatives that were not acted upon; yet the side which gained ascendancy often did so by a slender margin, and only bad luck may have prevented those who supported different ideas from succeeding. Since history pays so little heed to what did not prevail, there is an illusion that what occurred in the past not only was deliberate but possessed some element of inevitability. This creates the impression that our times are more uncertain than earlier ones, and have a greater confusion of tongues.

Anyone with a long memory can recall how confident were widely-held expectations of settled peace in the early years of this century. They were so strong that canny Andrew Carnegie made provision for other uses of his Endowment for International Peace when it was no longer needed for the attainment of its original purpose. Belief in the prompt arrival of such a millennium was based upon what proved to be an overly naïve projection of what seemed like a trend; many complex and exceedingly powerful historical forces were not taken into account.

The factors involved in historical events are so numerous and so complicated that any explanation, however detailed, is an oversimplification—often so great as to be seriously misleading. The Senate investigating committee that took its name from the late Senator Nye of North Dakota assigned armament makers a major responsibility for the First World War. It was such an oversimplification as to constitute gross error. Yet for several years it had a marked influence upon public opinion and on actions of Congress.

In the second place, prophecies, regarding which there was broad agreement a generation ago, failed because the revolutionary scope and force of the scientific and technological explosion were not foreseen. Imminent shortages of coal and oil, the rapid exhaustion of other natural resources, the stabilization of population, these and many other "inevitabilities" were taught to youth, and accepted by them as verities. They took form before Henry Ford made the automobile ubiquitous; just after the Wright brothers had lifted their frail powered kite off Kitty Hawk (to which, incidentally, contemporaries paid little heed); before oil and gas exploration had really become scientific; when atomic energy was no more than a fancy; before radio, television, and all the advances in communications. It is easily assumed that techniques have been so improved that such gross errors cannot now occur. Yet we are offered rather precise figures regarding the population of Red China in the year 2000, though we cannot be sure within 100,000,000 what it is today. Recall, also, the statistical nonsense that was visited upon us in the year of the "great leap forward" when every family in China was to make iron in the back yard. Now other statisticians have famine as a built-in characteristic of the regime.

The projection of trends into the future is more dangerous than helpful in a third decisive way. The human factors are so different from physical data that the assumption that events will follow a "normal curve" is incredible. So variable, so complex are the human factors that in deeply significant political matters the theory of probability breaks down. Who will be so bold as to foretell what will happen to the structure of French politics and government with the disappearence of de Gaulle? When so dominant a figure leaves the scene all is at hazard. On what foundation can one predict the decade of the seventies for Mexico, Brazil, Argentina? What is the future of Red China?

A sophisticated approach to tomorrow's world, therefore, will give little heed to overconfident predictions. The late Carl Becker—a historian of rare perception—summed up the reality in a single sentence: "In human affairs nothing is predetermined until after it has occurred." The form of his statement is what used to be called an Irish bull, but it is a profound observation nonetheless.

A more subtle and sophisticated approach will end the habit of feeling sorry for ourselves because difficulties are great. Historically two sorts of people have always been—and still are—excessively vocal. One group looks to the past and laments a lost golden age; the other looks to the future and promises a brave new world. Both groups have always agreed upon one thing, that their own times were out of joint.

These traits are old. In the sixth chapter of Genesis, no less, is the phrase, "There were giants in the earth in those days." An Assyrian tablet, dating from the third millennium B.C., bewails that "the earth is degenerating in these latter days. There are signs that the world is speedily coming to an end. Bribery and corruption abound. Children no longer obey their parents." Four hundred years before the Christian era one of the Greek dramatists wrote of earlier times: "Fortunate were they who lived then with our ancestors." The Utopians have been just as vocal, just as persistent, and just as wrong.

The world has always had troubles. Most major problems are as old as the hills. The basic quest for peace is coterminous with human history. In a recent issue of *Foreign Affairs*,[1] Senator Fulbright called for a concert of free nations. Cardinal Wolsey thought he had assured a concert of Europe for peace in the Treaty of 1518. The pressure of population distressed men long before Malthus. Taxes—how to pay the costs of government—have been the subject of bitter complaint for many centuries. The destructive power of new weapons has frightened successive generations. Famine and plague long seemed historically endemic. The list could be extended almost indefinitely. Failure to appreciate the antiquity of urgent issues is simply a measure of our ignorance of the past. Any era studied intensively would reveal periods of crisis, wars, hunger, pestilence, tyranny, slavery, poverty, and a host of other ills, most of which are lost to memory.

Beyond ignorance of the past there are four other reasons why we are so acutely aware of current crisis. The first is that weapons have attained a deadliness and a pace of development so great as to make war, always terrible, and long since a poor instrument of policy, seem conceivable only as a last and desperate resort. Like

[1] October 1961.

many other new concepts, this conclusion is new principally in being more widely held. After the First World War, Winston Churchill wrote: "Victory was to be bought so dear as to be almost indistinguishable from defeat. It was not to give security even to the victors." His judgment was seconded by Aristide Briand who said: "In modern war there is no victor. Defeat reaches out its heavy hand to the uttermost corners of the earth, and lays its burdens on victor and vanquished alike."

The second reason for the heightened sense of crisis is that we have developed a greater sensitiveness to poverty, unemployment, and ill health. Trespasses upon the individual personality to which the world was long callous now evoke a sense of outrage. The passing of colonialism is a manifestation of respect for the rights of man; domination of one group over another, even "for its own good," involves an abuse that we no longer wish to tolerate.

The third reason why modern troubles seem acute is that the miracles of communication make us constantly aware of them. Every hour on the hour ills of the world of which our fathers remained blissfully ignorant are dinned into our ears and every morning are piled on our doorsteps.

Fourthly, we have had so many successes—from the conquest of tuberculosis, polio, and many other diseases to the elimination of famine and the mitigation of poverty (for even our destitute are well-off compared with the poor of Asia)—that we feel frustrated when we cannot find a prompt remedy for every ill to which man is heir.

We should remember that as the scale of our difficulties has risen the resources available to meet them have also increased enormously. It is because we are rich and powerful, with world-wide interests, that the troubles of Southeast Asia or West Africa harass us. But who would revert to the days of our poverty and isolation in order to escape the cares that now concern us?

For more than two centuries after the colonization of this continent we paid little attention to faraway lands and strange people. Subduing the wilderness was enough to occupy most of our energies. Nonetheless, individuals ventured afar; whalers and traders made contacts. They expanded their activities for many years before the government took action in their support.

In 1832 a New Hampshire sea captain, familiar with the perils of American shipping in Asiatic waters, persuaded the State Department that we should have treaties of friendship and commerce so that crews of wrecked vessels, and other Americans who fell upon misfortune, should not be abused. He was furnished some passports, a sheaf of letters of credence, and full powers to negotiate such treaties, at a stipend of six dollars a day. The names of countries to which he was to go and the names and titles of their rulers were left blank; he was to fill them in himself. The reason was stated with refreshing candor: "The titles appertaining to their majesties . . . [are] unknown here." Though the naïveté of such a proceeding brings a smile, it nevertheless was adequate for its day. Now, not only have our interests in those parts become immensely more important, but there is dramatic change in the sensitivity of the rulers. It will no longer suffice to confess an amiable ignorance; that would be taken as a deadly insult. A seasoned knowledge of every area is essential.

That prescription is easy to put into words; to put it into practice is a task of monumental proportions in many parts of the world. Language offers a convenient illustration of the difficulty. It is frequently urged that our diplomatic representatives should know the language of the country where they are assigned; but often there is no "language of the country." In one large and strategically significant nation there are said to be two hundred languages, twenty "principal" ones. Even if the diplomat learns to converse with official circles, he is still cut off from the mass of the population.

There are other difficulties that confront us when we seek to understand the newer nations with which we are called upon to deal today. In several cases linguistic barriers retard the development of true nationhood. In some advanced nations, such as Switzerland, that particular divisive force is overcome by other stronger forces of unity. But in the newer and undeveloped countries, where education has lagged, the countervailing forces are weak or nonexistent. Thus many of the countries with which we must deal are not nations at all in the sense we understand the term. Though in the United Nations they may speak in tones of aggressive nationalism, domestically the government may have only titular control of large areas.

Cultural diversity intensifies the difficulty of attaining true nationhood. Even in mature countries, forces of separatism often persist. Our neighbor, Canada, despite its ardent national spirit, is compelled to pay careful deference to the reality of its two cultures. Scotland and Wales have shown a marked increase in self-consciousness which in its extreme forms amounts to nationalism. The deep cleavages between Flemings and Walloons in Belgium have been dangerously manifest in recent years. If such phenomena can be found in countries where the reality of nationhood is beyond challenge, how much more likely are they to be found in new ones. In some parts of Africa, for example, fidelity to the tribe is so much stronger than attachment to the state that the concept of a nation has little meaning. Cultural diversities produce strains not only in Africa but in India, Ceylon, Indonesia, Malaya, and several Latin American countries.

Cultural forces, moreover, are not governed by economic interests; indeed, they are virtually impervious to them. They may even be intensified when all the economic inducements call for unity. This is a significant limitation upon the leverage that can be exercised by money, through foreign aid or investment. Programs of assistance are not only made more difficult; there is always danger that they may exacerbate internal stresses already severe enough to imperil the integrity of the country.

On top of linguistic and cultural cleavages, there frequently is a sharp dichotomy in the national economic structure. Oil, minerals, and other natural resources may produce great wealth side by side with rudimentary industry and primitive agricultural techniques. It would be logical that the wealth produced by one sector of the economy should be used to stimulate and improve the others. But since history is not a mirror of logic, the record is quite different.

To render changes in this situation even more difficult, economic divisions tend to coincide with and accentuate ethnic, linguistic, and cultural divisions. In the same nation one may often find a highly cultivated level of society existing cheek by jowl with depths of ignorance and degradation. In developed countries there has gradually come about a kind of moral revolution, so that when such situations are found to exist an acute sense of guilt appears and with it a demand for reform. But just as the industrial and agricultural revolutions bypassed the undeveloped nations so also did the moral—or social—revolution, with the result that in many of them there has never emerged an indigenous urge or method for reform. Indeed, bitter resistance to the creation of a more nearly unified society appears at both the highest and the lowest levels; the reasons are different, but the reluctance to change persists.

These are some of the realities—many more could be mentioned—which we must understand when we seek to help these nations. For us to be useful we must be wise in addition to being well-intentioned. Our mission is a far cry from Edmund Roberts' treaty-making in Southeast Asia in 1832, when a rough knowledge based on rugged experience sufficed. Today, besides detailed knowledge and learning, we must have enough imagination to enable us to enter into the experience of people of different ethnic origin, cultural heritage, and economic experience.

It is hard enough to grasp one culture, much less to become an expert in many. This does not mean, however, that we can turn matters over to an elite corps of experts, and relax. We must all come to appreciate that many things valid for us are not necessarily adapted to the needs, or the minds, of others. While some nations want desperately some things which we have, other things we hold in highest regard they do not want at all. And it is the quintessence of naïveté to expect that people with histories radically different from ours will necessarily accept our political, social, economic, and ethical values.

Indeed, our maturity in international affairs can be measured by the patience with which we tolerate preachments, however galling, on the virtues of "noncommitment" and the vices of "imperialism." In the United Nations and in other forums the spokesmen of various nations often affect a moral elevation, not to say superiority, that ill accords with some of their domestic behavior and their attitudes toward neighboring (particularly weaker) countries. A sense of humor and a remembrance of history will help. One can find many parallel statements by spokesmen of the United States in the days of our weakness; our politicians long delighted to twist the lion's tail and had warm popular support in so doing.

Factors of prime importance make programs of foreign aid inevitable and far outweigh the difficulties mentioned. Nonetheless, the difficulties do indicate that expectations of rapid and dramatic success will often prove unfounded. At best, setbacks are inescapable and must be accepted, if not with resignation, at least philosophically.

It will not do to cry "failure" when we see the military, often the only disciplined body of public servants existing in a new and inexperienced country, purge corrupt men from office and attack flagrant nepotism. Nor should we be astonished when opposition leaders are thrust into jail, or tried and executed. Social change that is both rapid and peaceful has been rare in history.

Attempts from the outside to prevent such upheavals are almost surely doomed to failure. Hoping to ward off catastrophic violence, President Wilson adopted the principle that we would not recognize new governments erected on the ruins of those overthrown by force. The policy was benevolent in intent but it was a failure; indeed, it did much to stimulate Latin American insistence upon the principle of nonintervention in its most extreme form. Benevolent purpose proved no match for political realities. The reason is not far to seek; static and inflexible societies tend to fracture under pressure. Men who had lived in an inherited status no longer "knew their place" when that status was reformed.

The phase of violence which social change almost inevitably precipitates opens the way for extremists to attain influence. The demagogue knows how to exploit those who have lost their social and economic moorings. Ortega y Gasset summed up the matter concisely: "As men lose confidence in and enthusiasm for their culture, they are, so to speak, left hanging in midair and incapable of opposing anyone who affirms anything.... Hence there are periods in which it is enough only to give a shout, no matter how arbitrary its phrasing, for everyone to surrender themselves to it."[2] It requires the utmost subtlety and skill to ride out such storms, and to promote democratic solutions rather than dictatorship or oligarchy.

Land reform is one of the inevitable concomitants of the social change we seek to stimulate. It is a convenient slogan, but does not constitute a program. Every nation requires a different prescription, carefully compounded to meet its own needs; even highly developed nations do not yet have an answer to their own problems, much less a generalized answer for all. West Germany, for example, has many small, uneconomic farms, cultivated by primitive means, subsidized by the state. The United States also has acute unresolved problems of land utilization. If highly organized and vigorous economies have not found ways and means to meet their problems, an

[2] *Man and Crisis,* New York, 1958.

attempt from the outside to counsel or impose solutions in an underdeveloped country, bound tightly by tradition and without adequate political institutions, is vastly more difficult. Simple, "obvious" solutions may do more harm than good. Americans should remember the slogan of the War Between the States, "forty acres and a mule," as a cure for the aftereffects of slavery. A man who is given the transient satisfactions of land ownership may thereafter suffer the ills of too small holdings and lack of capital for seed, fertilizer, and machinery; he may be without the necessary training to be an independent operator and may have no ready market, or if one is available, may lack market experience.

In dispensing aid we must not be unduly shocked if corruption is a concomitant. The concept of public office as a public trust grows slowly and never attains perfection, as our own record shows. When a relatively large amount of money is poured into a poverty-stricken country we would be naïve to expect that all of it will be used wisely. Waste is especially likely to occur where there is no corps of trained civil servants and no deeply rooted sense of public responsibility.

Necessary as aid is, the course to be steered between cooperation (the professed aim) and intervention (a hated word) is narrow and slippery in the extreme. The road can be negotiated, if at all, only if there is complete correspondence between profession and performance.

The great objective of the Alliance for Progress is to encourage the development of a continent in such a way that land and learning, opportunity and culture, property and power will be more widely and more fairly distributed. We hope to see formed the substance of democracy, not a sham façade for oligarchy or dictatorship.

For that noble objective to be attained, social and economic reforms are required. In making reforms a *sine qua non* of aid, we often forget—it is never forgotten by the recipients—that the United States will be the judge of their adequacy. The language of diplomacy should not conceal that this constitutes a sort of intervention in the internal affairs of Latin America—beneficent in purpose, potentially useful in result, but intervention nonetheless.

This lays upon the United States two obligations. The first is to know the characteristics and needs of each country, not to lump them together as though the differences between them were not profound. That, alone, is an exacting requirement not as yet met. The second is to maintain the integrity of the project, to use it for its stated purpose and for no other, however desirable another may appear at the moment. This is not a counsel of perfection so much as a severely practical necessity. Strict fidelity to the announced principles of the Marshall Plan was a primary ingredient of its brilliant success. At the Punta del Este meeting of Foreign Ministers,[3] unhappily, members of the United States delegation intimated that lack of strong resolutions such as Washington desired might have an adverse effect upon the size of the appropriations which Congress might grant. The hint, or threat, constituted a use of the program not for its declared purpose of assisting domestic reform but to spur adoption of an international position desired by the United States. This tended to impair the integrity of the program by making it an instrument in the cold war. Surely this was a failure to understand the psychology of essential partners in the enterprise.

---

[3] January 22-31, 1962.

The history of our attitude to alliances is instructive today. At the outset of our struggle for independence we eagerly sought help abroad. It was one of the triumphs of Benjamin Franklin's diplomacy that he exploited France's troubles with England to obtain a treaty of alliance with France in 1778, the declared purpose of which was thus expressed: "The essential and direct end of the present defensive alliance is to maintain effectually the liberty, sovereignty, and independence absolute and unlimited, of the said United States, as well in matters of government as of commerce." What a modern sound it has! That alliance was a vital factor in the success of the Revolution.

After the war, the interests of the United States diverged from those of France, which wanted to continue to use the United States as a pawn in its power struggle with England. Before the end of Washington's first administration, Vice President John Adams wrote: "America has been long enough involved with wars of Europe. She has been a football between contending nations from the beginning, and it is easy to foresee that France and England will both endeavor to involve us in their future wars. It is our interest and duty to avoid them as much as possible, and to be completely independent, and to have nothing to do with either of them, but in commerce."

Our Declaration of Neutrality was issued the next year, and in 1796 came the classic statements in Washington's Farewell Address: It is "unwise in us to implicate ourselves by artificial ties in the ordinary vicissitudes of her [Europe's] politics or the ordinary combinations and collisions of her friendships or enmities." And again: "It is our true policy to steer clear of permanent alliances with any portion of the foreign world. . . . We may safely trust to temporary alliances for extraordinary emergencies."

Circumstances were such that no further alliances were made by the men who shaped our government under the Constitution. With the passage of time, key words in Washington's statements were forgotten: he did not denounce all alliances, only permanent ones; he specifically endorsed temporary alliances. His qualifying expressions were overlooked; such subtleties were lost to memory. In the public mind all alliances became entangling.

The fact that we did not participate in other alliances kept us from appreciating that our unhappy experience with France after the immediate objective had been attained was more nearly normal than unusual. We never learned to appreciate how brittle alliances have customarily been, how frequently nations have changed partners even in the midst of critical times.

The century and more of a hardening mood against any alliance under any circumstances whatever deprived the United States of an important element of flexibility in policy. The rigidity went so far that during the First World War Woodrow Wilson would not so much as use the word "ally" colloquially; he insisted upon referring to our "associates." Franklin Roosevelt spoke of alliances colloquially, but signed no treaties. In retrospect it seems almost incredible that because of the hard mold in which our mental processes had become fixed we should have failed to make terms for our participation in two world wars.

Since we lacked experience with alliances and had failed to learn at first hand what they could and could not do, we were in difficulties also when policy was reversed and alliances were made during President Truman's administration. There then tended to be a complete reversal of mood also. Just as alliances had long seemed synonymous with evil, they now were identified with good; as before there had been extravagant fears of entanglement, there now were extravagant hopes of cooperation.

There is urgent need for fresh and perceptive analysis of what can reasonably be expected of alliances and what cannot. They arise less often from a real cohesion of common interests among nations fairly equal in power than from a common danger. Nearly all alliances are proclaimed as defensive; the most successful are usually those which are in fact defensive in the face of real and pressing dangers.

Alliances should not be sentimentalized. Washington's warnings against "permanent, inveterate antipathies" and "passionate attachment of one nation for another" are still valid. Our postwar relationships with Germany and Japan illustrate our ability to resist a temptation to permanent antipathies. We must not expect permanent attachments either; even our "special relationship" with Britain must never be taken for granted. Our war and postwar contacts with Russia never did involve a passionate attachment, but we must now beware of the permanent antipathy described by Washington lest it some day prevent us from taking advantage of possible, however unforeseen, changes in the Soviet character or position.

Alliances are sometimes called "marriages of convenience," but that is too sweeping a metaphor. They are better considered as limited partnerships for specific purposes for a relatively short time—as short as the attainment of the specific objective permits. The reason for this can be simply stated, though to operate within the limitations set may well be infinitely complicated. All significant international intercourse involves some surrender of freedom of action, and it is inevitably greater in the case of an alliance; for the outcome is shaped not only by what we do but also by what the other participant does. Though we act with the wisdom of serpents, if the other acts foolishly the consequence may be as disastrous for us as though we had been foolish too.

The difficulties and risks are compounded when responsibility is shared not merely bilaterally but multilaterally; then one nation, acting wrongheadedly or without adequate skill, may wreck the efforts of all the others. And the chances of error resulting in failure are multiplied not arithmetically but geometrically when responsibility is shared not over one but over several areas of interest. One power can wreck many aspects of the work of several nations. Moreover, the likelihood of internal strains within the alliance also advances geometrically. Even two nations never have a uniformity of interest. Thus despite our close connection with Britain, British views with regard to Red China (to take a single example) contrast sharply with ours. In a group alliance the tensions among conflicting interests, real or imagined, mount rapidly. Not only the substance of policy but the manner of approach grow in complexity. There is always danger that some nation's ideas will not be heard with enough attention to avoid wounding its *amour propre*. This difficulty is compounded when the alliance is between states of markedly unequal size and resources—the usual situation. The less powerful are acutely conscious that wisdom is not distributed in direct proportion to power. Successful participation in a multiple alliance thus requires self-discipline and patience beyond that demanded in ordinary international intercourse.

These considerations do not constitute an argument against alliances but they do suggest the unwisdom of extending alliances to more nations than is absolutely necessary. They also constitute an argument against the feeling that the way to strengthen an existing alliance is to load it with new and different functions. When an alliance has fulfilled its basic mission and rough relationships have been smoothed, there may be reason for adding to its responsibility. But when objectives are still beyond present attainment and internal strains are evident it is not the best time to add new and more complex obligations.

Many of these same considerations apply to our participation in international organizations. In the public mind, international organizations were long equated with alliances. The United States was a prime mover in the establishment of an international court, then abstained from participation in it for many years, and finally joined with a reservation that made our commitment highly equivocal. The United States demanded and helped to shape the League of Nations, and then declined to participate; the halls of Congress rang with the word "entanglement." We thereby lost the experience in international organization that participation in the League would have supplied. As a nonparticipant we found it easy to hold others responsible for the League's failure.

Lacking experience, we supposed that the United Nations would do better with our participation and under our leadership. Have not the events of the last fifteen years shown that we entered it with higher expectations than could reasonably be fulfilled? In retrospect, it is painfully clear that a key premise was false: the structure of the organization rested upon a presumption of continued unity among the five great powers that had led the victorious coalition. Tensions during the war should have alerted us to the fragility of that hope.

As long as there was, in effect, an automatic majority for the Western position, the difficulties arising from the failure of the great powers to cooperate were serious, but no more. With the admission of over fifty new nations (and more coming), many of them totally inexperienced, and with the growth of the attitude of noncommitment in all its various shades of definition, the complexities involved in utilizing the United Nations as a major instrument of policy begin to emerge. Already we have hedged by setting up organizations related to the United Nations but not immediately under it. It is now plain that our participation in this international forum calls for more perception and delicacy than we realized at the start, or even five years ago.

We encouraged another type of international organization without becoming affiliated; the Coal and Steel Community and the Common Market are two illustrations. After the war the economies of Europe were in physical ruin or in a state of demoralization. The Marshall Plan gave a great thrust to their recovery. As part of our effort to get Europe on its feet, the United States pressed for the reduction of barriers to international trade and the development of larger tariff-free markets. The Common Market advanced both aims. Today the rate of economic growth in Western Europe exceeds that of the United States and Britain. Whereas for years the world complained of a dollar gap, we now find the two principal trading currencies of the world—the dollar and the pound—under severe pressure. There is now a dollar deficiency, and it is possible that competition from the Common Market countries may well make the cure of this situation more difficult. The trading patterns of the world are shifting dramatically; old habits and ideas are no longer really "conservative"; many are simply irrelevant.

The need for deeper understanding in this matter is great. The traditional way out of exchange difficulties is to resort to protectionism in one of its many forms. That was our approach in the nineteenth and early twentieth centuries. In the world of tomorrow such a course might give momentary relief to a few industries but would surely bring ultimate disaster. We have promoted the new organizations; they have thus far done better than all expectations; we must now find ways to work with them either as an active partner or as an effective competitor. The British have elected to apply for admission to the Common Market as the least troublesome among several alternatives, each of them filled with difficulty. At the moment such a course of action is probably not appropriate for us. But tomorrow will require new policies, and it may be that radical actions will be the most genuinely conservative by preserving key values in drastically changed circumstances.

The thesis that in our days policy in action must be increasingly subtle and sophisticated could have been illustrated in many ways besides the six selected. No matter how many were used, however, all would emphasize the central reality that subtlety and sophistication are human traits, not governed by the dramatic developments in the physical world. Startling changes in our temporal environment do dramatize the necessity for more profound learning, keener perception, heightened sensitivity, and all the other ingredients of sophistication. But they likewise demonstrate that there has been no break in the continuity of history, of human experience.

No good purpose is served by fostering the illusion that we live in a "new age." Distinctive eras are identified and get their accepted names long after they are past, seldom or never from contemporaries. At best the concept of an age remains imprecise, and even when historians reach some agreement upon a name—say the Renaissance—the dates assigned by different scholars to its onset and its passing will vary a century or more at either end. Similarly there will be dispute as to which of its characteristics are the essential ones.

We must be on our guard, too, against seeing incidents, however catastrophic, as "decisive," against assigning permanent significance to events which are momentarily prominent but when seen in perspective are found to have been transient in effect. On one occasion Disraeli exclaimed: "Not a principle in the management of our foreign affairs, accepted by all statesmen for guidance up to six months ago, exists. . . . You have a new world. . . . The balance of power has been entirely destroyed." Today, only a professional historian would know what Disraeli was talking about, and he would also know that Disraeli was wrong. Disraeli had let a catastrophic event warp his judgment. This tendency to exaggerate the importance of current events is characteristic of all eras, but it is heightened in ours by the speed and the dramatic impact provided by modern communications. "This, too, will pass away" is an ancient saying, but as true and as relevant as ever.

For humans who wrestle with events in the attempt to shape their own destiny, any form of determinism should be incredible. It is also the deadly enemy of our political philosophy. The drives that activate men are fundamental and continuous, but their direction and intensity vary not only from age to age, but from moment to moment, and from man to man. That is why we no longer hear the deterministic slogan "manifest destiny," though it was long a popular fetish; that is why Hitler's inevitable "wave of the future" is broken. Khrushchev appeals to "scientific history"—itself a contradiction in terms—as proof of the ultimate triumph of Communism. If it triumphs it will not be because it is "inevitable" but because our policy in action lacks subtlety and sophistication.

It may have been noticed that thus far no mention has been made of power in a time when the phrase "power politics" has become fashionable once again. Indeed, there is a plain inference in much current discussion that power is the principal ingredient in international affairs. Power obviously has its place, and in some phases of policy—such as dealing between equals—it is a major factor. But there are few equals among nations of the world, and paradoxically our time is marked more by the baiting and bullying of the strong by the weak than by the control of small powers by the great ones. In the Russian orbit, of course, naked force is often used to maintain ascendancy, as witness Hungary and East Germany. But in the rest of the world the mere possession of power tends to put those who possess it on the defensive. It is not a lack of power on the part of the colonial nations that is precipitating the liquidation of their empires, but forces essentially quite different. In our own case, we find our relationship with the states of Latin America made infinitely more complicated because the disparity in physical power between them and us is so conspicuous. The Giant of the North is feared just because it is so powerful, and fear easily slides into distrust and dislike.

In our day, as I have tried to show, all the elements entering into successful international policy and action require a more sophisticated understanding than ever before. For those who possess power, the manner in which they use it is perhaps the element requiring subtlety in the highest degree.

IX ∽ The Primacy of Secondary Consequences

IN RESPONSE to an emergency summons, a number of possible topics floated across my mind. After reflection, I decided to work off an old frustration. For twenty years or more I have been trying to give a speech, but have never been able to write it; no matter how much rhetorical pectin I threw into the pot, it just would not jell. Mountains of material accumulated—some too green, some overripe. Today, having thrown away all that material, I shall give it even if it remains stubbornly liquid.

I propose to speak of "the primacy of secondary consequences," and shall follow a procedure the reverse of the old Scotch preacher. He told his congregation: "I am about to deal with a deeficult matter. I shall approach it carefully, and then go around it." I am going to circumnavigate the topic for a few moments, then head straight into it.

The difference between a politician and a statesman can be put in these terms: in a dilemma the politician

---
Edward Lamb Award for Excellence in Management, Columbia University, May 29, 1962.

tries to wriggle his way between the horns, using lots of grease, but avoiding the sharp points. Then when he has slipped through, smeared indeed and somewhat tattered, he claims to have preserved the public interest. In reality he has left the beastie with his horns intact ready to impale the next person who approaches him. A statesman, on the contrary, seizes the dilemma, wrestles it into submission, and dehorns it. Thereafter it may snort and paw the ground, but its capacity for damage is gone.

In short, the politician is concerned with the primary consideration—getting by *this* time. The statesman takes into account the secondary consequences—the ultimate effect as well as escape from the immediate crisis.

Usually the secondary consequences become obvious only slowly; they may be so long deferred that the public has forgotten, and the politician escapes the unhappy results. But not always. In September 1938, Neville Chamberlain came back from Munich after conceding all Hitler's demands. With the sententiousness which is the politician's great asset, he told the crowd in Downing Street: I bring you "peace in our time." He was greeted with acclaim, for peace is always the hope of the public. He had achieved his primary goal of slipping between the horns of the dilemma, but had avoided the real issue.

War was only postponed, and not for long—just one year until September 1939. Meanwhile the false sense of security had kept Britain from making adequate preparations for the great catastrophe that was to come. Thus his evasion of the issue compounded the disaster when it struck. He who had been so wildly acclaimed now suffered humiliation. In May 1940, one of his own party, a long-time friend and associate in Birmingham, rose in Parliament and quoted Cromwell's injunction to the Long

Parliament: "Depart, I say, and let us have done with you. In the name of God, go!" In his last decisive intervention in parliamentary affairs, the fiery old Lloyd George, who had been such a force in the First World War, was equally explicit: "I say solemnly that the Prime Minister should give an example of sacrifice, because there is nothing which can contribute more to victory in this war than that he should sacrifice the seals of office."

Sometimes, however, the secondary effects are so slow in maturing, or are so subtle, that they never come to wide public notice though they lack neither substance nor significance. Let us choose another British example. To meet acute monetary and exchange problems after the Second World War severe restrictions were put upon the amount of money that could be spent on travel abroad. It helped, presumably, to achieve the primary objective, though it was only one straw in a whole haystack of measures, the precise effect of any one of which cannot be disentangled from the rest.

Now the secondary consequences begin to appear. Britain finds it essential to create a new relationship with Europe. This involves, inescapably, a new relationship with the independent nations of the Commonwealth. It also entails a new relationship with the United States.

In that vast and complicated series of readjustments all 'round the world, Britain needs not only skilled diplomats and civil servants, but many businessmen who know with real intimacy—at first hand—what are the realities in the far reaches of the earth, not just what is occurring in the tight little isle, which is getting into a tighter corner moment by moment. It needs, also, leaders of public opinion who have direct familiarity with situations abroad.

A long-concealed secondary effect of the protracted

restrictions on travel is that Britain has bred a generation of businessmen who, taking it by and large, have not seen the world. Too many were denied, by government restrictions, opportunity to acquire that first hand knowledge so essential to drastic reconstruction of their affairs in order to meet with a fair chance of success the aggressive competition of others who possess such intimate knowledge.

There is an element of unconscious humor, but with bitter overtones, in the offhand remark of a businessman in Britain only three weeks ago. "Of course," he said, "if Britain enters the Common Market the principal currency will be the pound sterling." The comment was not that of a stupid man, but of one long denied, through no fault of his own, an essential element in his practical education through experience.

I have drawn these illustrations of secondary consequences from Britain. This is not because blindness to ultimate effects has been a special characteristic of that nation. Our own record furnishes illustrations just as dramatic, on the one hand, and just as subtle, on the other. But there might have been some feeling, on the part of someone, that partisan considerations had dictated the choice of examples.

Having circumnavigated the problem, I now propose to head directly into its relevance to business. As the politician who avoids the real issue can be distinguished from the statesman who faces it, so, also, it is possible to classify businessmen.

Recently at an American Assembly session on Automation at Arden House, great stress was laid by many people upon the vital necessity for research if we are to stay competitive with nations whose economies are growing at a faster rate than ours—particularly in view of our uniquely high wage rates. One participant reacted away from this conclusion. During the coffee-break he came to me, though I was a nonparticipant, and cited one great corporation that had decided against research and automation. It had a well-developed market and put its energies into serving that market, disregarding export and other opportunities. It has consistently made a profit and has met its dividend requirements. What, the dissenter demanded, with some heat, was wrong with that? My answer was: "Nothing, for the moment. But for the long pull it would be so disastrous that I would not touch the stock with a ten-foot pole." To my astonishment the inquiring participant said, "If you put it that way, I agree with you." Here is an instance where the primary objective, current profit, is being attained. The secondary consequence, in the light of the new intensity of international competition, is likely to be disastrous.

A classic instance of failure to take account of secondary consequences involved both our government and the leaders of business. It occurred long enough ago so that the major participants are no longer in posts of authority. Thus the matter can be looked at calmly, and in perspective. It was the National Industrial Recovery Act which became law on June 16, 1933. It might well have been called the National Act of Desperation.

In so describing it, fairness requires us to recognize that there was occasion for men to feel some measure of desperation. One of the most distinguished historians America ever produced set down some facts now but dimly remembered: "Twenty million men without jobs and without hope for the future; farmers with crops rotting on the ground and no remedy in sight except to limit the production of foodstuffs; labor unions discredited by gangster tactics and businessmen in a mood to 'smash the unions' at all costs; class conflicts too embittered to be reconciled and pressure politics too unrestrained to be joked about; a 'bundles for congress' movement sweeping the country."[1]

Despite the great distinction of the author, that picture now seems overdrawn. But his words were written in 1944, while the memories of the great depression were still acutely vivid. And the mood of the times is as real a historical fact as names, places, and dates, for history is not recorded in a vacuum. It reflects the spirit of the age in which it is written; and that passage accurately reflects the dominant mood. The "mature economy" was on the lips of virtually every economist; "our industrial plant is built" was the dogma of the President. A distinguished panel of citizens, under the chairmanship of one of the most famous of our great industrialists, reported that we were turning out not only too many young people with college degrees, but too many high school graduates.

That atmosphere of disillusionment and discouragement produced an astounding alliance. The political leader was generally regarded as the furthest left of all our Presidents. The business community was dominated by men of conservative bent. Seldom has the tension between the President and businessmen been more acute. Yet they united in hailing the National Industrial Recovery Act. An official review, transmitted to the Congress with a Presidential Message, described it accurately as a "radical experiment in incorporating interested economic groups as agencies of government."

---

[1] Carl L. Becker, *How New Will the Better World Be,* New York, 1944.

They had their eyes upon the immediate problem—escaping the constricting coils of the great depression. So intense was their fascination with that immediate objective that businessmen who had been fighting unionization accepted the famous labor clause, 7a, which resulted in a tenfold increase in union membership in the mass-production industries. It offered John L. Lewis an opportunity to announce in his own sonorous way: "The President wants you to join a union."

Men to whom that dogma was an anathema nonetheless put the blue eagle in their windows, and entered with enthusiasm into the construction and administration of so-called "fair-trade codes." These, when approved by the President, were enforceable as law. One of the trustees of an institution I was then administering expressed his delight at the opportunity the code offered. He said, in substance: "Now no one can set up a mill to make my product without a certificate of convenience and necessity. I am on the board that would issue such a certificate; let anyone try to get one!" He had exchanged freedom for a false security and had no awareness of what he had surrendered. It was a profoundly impressive demonstration of how myopic normally farsighted people can become in a time of crisis.

Within less than a year[2] the National Recovery Review Board reported that the NRA was stimulating monopoly practices and that cartelization was proceeding apace. This occurred despite the fact that the Act had given pious lip service to the basic American docrine that codes "shall not permit monopolies or monopolistic practices," or "eliminate or oppress small enterprises." One secondary effect of the NRA has lingered to this day—and

---

[2] May 2, 1934.

I am going to refer to it more than once—namely, a popular suspicion that business is not really competitive, but is under the domination of monopolists or quasi monopolists.

The NRA revealed a demonstrable drift toward the Corporative State—a name Mussolini devised after the fact to give the illusion of rationality to his raw empiricism. We must remember that, in like manner, the NRA was not the product of theorists deviously seeking to commit the nation to a managed economy. It was shaped by "practical men," politicians and industrialists who knew so little theory that they did not recognize obvious similarities to Fascism. It was businessmen who were promoting a planned economy.

The very next year, on May 27, 1935, the Supreme Court, composed, as President Roosevelt scornfully said, of "nine old men" who belonged in the "horse and buggy" days, declared the NRA unconstitutional in the famous "chicken case." The whole phantasmagoria had lasted a little less than two years. It failed in its primary purpose; but some of its secondary effects have not yet disappeared.

I deliberately chose an illustration far enough back in history so that it could be looked at objectively, without passion. But it would be improper to avoid current issues. Last week President Kennedy called together industrialists, union leaders, and academics for a White House Conference on national issues. He besought the conferees to lay aside partisanship, preconceptions, philosophical labels, and bring fresh thought to current issues.

In all candor it must be admitted he set no model in that regard. He returned to an old argument, familiar in the thirties, that great issues are essentially technical and so sophisticated as not to be within the comprehension of the ordinary citizen. It was the sort of reasoning that earlier produced the rage for Technocracy—briefly, heaven be praised. He then seemed to abandon the technocratic argument and asked the diverse group to work together to find solutions. No sooner had he concluded his appeal, however, than there ensued, for the most part, a series of the old stylized—not to say stale—arguments.

Charles P. Taft did, however, raise one basic issue—the participation of the consumer in improved production through price reductions. Secretary of the Treasury Dillon gave incidental support to that view. That this aspect of our economic life should have had so little attention is astonishing, for the classic argument on behalf of the American brand of capitalism has been that owners, workers, *and customers* should share the benefits of the system. But all too often the customer has been the forgotten man in the triumvirate.

Let me illustrate. Some years ago there was a significant breakthrough in collective bargaining. Wages were tied to the cost of living index. The immediate benefits were clear; the contract brought a measure of industrial peace; it shielded workers under it against the inflationary erosion of their real incomes. The person who did not benefit was the consumer. The secondary effect was that the new arrangement gave a nudge to the cost-price spiral. Whatever the government did, or failed to do, that increased inflation, this contract made matters still worse for the consumer who faced higher prices.

Take another instance. Earlier I alluded to the secondary effect of the NRA in promoting the idea that business is not really competitive, that prices are administered rather than the result of free competition. In recent years the public has seen wages and prices rise in the steel industry, while, simultaneously, unemployment and unused capacity were also increasing. This looked to the public suspiciously like administered prices. The public knew that governmental power, not economic forces, controls basic prices of sugar, wheat, corn, cotton, zinc, silver, and many other products. Now it had the feeling that an exercise of economic power, not free market forces, was determining prices in a basic commodity. Whether that was an accurate estimate of the situation is not nearly so significant as the existence of the widespread impression, for people act on what they think are the facts.

This accounts, in my judgment, for the public attitude when the President, in an overt display of power, forced a standstill in steel prices. The business world is manifestly unhappy at such forceful, not to say forcible, political intervention in pricing. It seems equally clear that general public opinion supported the action of the President. That is the secondary effect of the long-developing feeling upon the part of the public that the consumer has not had an equitable share in the benefits of better productivity. There was an underlying resentment at the long continuance of the cost-price push. A belief that neither management nor labor was concerned enough with his interests led the consumer to accept government intervention. He felt that if power, rather than a free market, is to determine prices, it had better be public, rather than private, power.

Now, however, a secondary effect of government intervention appears, and I must emphasize that this speech was written Saturday, before yesterday's dramatic events.[3] Prices of stocks are set in a *relatively* free market. If

---
[3] The sharp break in stock prices, May 28, 1962.

governmental power is to determine not only what share of profits it will take in taxes, but is also to set basic prices, and hence profits, confidence in equity values is shaken. Stock prices always overdiscount the future. When there is an ebullient feeling, men will pay forty to fifty times earnings for "growth" stocks. When confidence ebbs, they are tempted to pay less than the liquidating value of the enterprise.

Let us now spend a moment with the newest fad, current here and in Britain: we are to curb the wage-price spiral by the dogma that wages should not rise faster than productivity. This new gospel has some of the virtues and all the vices of oversimplification. Since a general average is used, no account is taken of the base line in any given industry or profession. That is why teachers, nurses, and others are so unhappy in Britain. Moreover, the formula neglects the source of the production increase —whether from new investment in better equipment, improved management, or a more productive labor force.

In any event, it has a further built-in fatal defect: the customer is forgotten. If this new "guide line"—the fashionable words for a governmental quasi directive—is followed, the alienation of the public will continue. Then political officers will be more and more tempted to represent their views as an adequate definition of the public interest. Regulation will proliferate, and Parkinson's Law will get fresh vindication.

Why have I laid such iterative stress upon the necessity for business to take account of secondary effects? The answer is startling. This generation of Americans has learned for the first time that freedom and enterprise are not indissolubly linked. Contrary to our traditional belief, enterprise not only can be, it has been, dynamic in the absence of freedom.

Hitler had the willing support of many great industrialists. Under the Nazis there was a vigorous recovery from the disastrous inflation of the Weimar regime. A potent industrial machine was built concurrently with the powerful military force. There were scientific and technological advances in many fields—that in rocketry nearly tipped the scales in the war. Under the tyranny of Communism the Soviets have grown into a mighty industrial and commercial force. Education, of its kind, has burgeoned; science—including medical science—has made remarkable advances; technology has shown sensational gains. Before the Second World War, under the domination of a military clique, Japan became a great industrial power and a commercial and fiscal competitor of formidable dimensions.

In the face of these demonstrations we can no longer assert that experience has shown that freedom is the only road to successful enterprise. Therefore, if business is to enjoy the vast benefits of freedom, it must identify the public interest with its own. When an industrialist asserts that his concern is to produce goods at a profit, he is stating less than half the truth; he is forgetting the vital secondary effects.

Historically American business has been radical; it has been a powerful revolutionary force. Eli Whitney's cotton gin produced not only economic results but vast social consequences. Every technological advance since has had secondary effects upon society far more significant than its primary economic impact.

Moreover, that revolution is accelerating. Thirty-three years ago, a group of colleagues and I sought to persuade a great industry to engage in research. It was hard, uphill work, but today research is the watchword in that industry. More was spent in the United States upon research last year than in all the period from the onset of the Industrial Revolution to the Second World War. To pretend that the impact of such a massive effort can be confined to economic life would be folly. That is why, in the last decade, corporate gifts to education, to cultural institutions, to hospitals, to United Funds, to the Red Cross have multiplied so rapidly. Industrial advance not only made leisure possible, but inevitable; now industry must participate in making leisure fruitful.

Business will be the whipping boy of the politician whenever its function is misrepresented as being aimed at profits alone. Profits it must have, as surely as a boiler must have fuel. But it must also have public appreciation and support which can come partly—but only partly—from an ever wider variety of products of better and better quality. There have been brilliant achievements in those respects in many fields, but the element of price must never be forgotten.

For all these reasons every decision must look beyond the visible and immediate to the invisible and deferred consequences. Secondary effects deserve primacy in thought. That is the definition of business statesmanship.